PETER SELG, specializing i atry and psy Wegman Ins Anthroposophy in Arlesheim, and the General Anthroposophical Section of the School of Spiritual Science (Goetheanum, Dornach). He teaches medical anthropology and ethics at the University of Witten/ Herdecke and the Alanus University of Arts and Social Sciences in Alfter, Germany. Peter Selg is the author of many dozens of books on anthroposophy.

2 m model, plaster cast, Edith Maryon and Rudolf Steiner, c. 1915/16. Reworked plaster cast with wire reinforcement, remains of plasticine (in the area of the being in the cave) and wooden board (to balance out the height of the central figure), 207 × 126 × 84 cm; scale 1:5. Taken from Mirela Faldey/David Hornemann v. Laer (editor): Im Spannungsfeld von Weltenkräften *('In the field of tension between cosmic forces')* Dornach 2020, page 61.

THE FUTURE
OF AHRIMAN

AND THE AWAKENING OF SOULS

The Spirit-Presence of the Mystery Dramas

Peter Selg

Translated by Paul King

TEMPLE LODGE

Temple Lodge Publishing Ltd.
Hillside House, The Square
Forest Row, RH18 5ES

www.templelodge.com

Published by Temple Lodge 2022

Originally published in German under the title *Die Zukunft Ahrimans und das 'Erwachen der Seelen', Zur Geistesgegenwart der Mysteriendramen* by Verlag am Goetheanum, Dornach, Switzer-land, 2021

© Verlag am Goetheanum, Dornach 2021
This translation © Temple Lodge Publishing 2022

A CIP catalogue record for this book is available from the British Library

ISBN 978 1 912230 87 7

Cover by Morgan Creative featuring image of Ahriman from a model by Rudolf Steiner (photograph by John Wilkes)
Typeset by Symbiosys Technologies, Visakhapatnam, India
Printed and bound by 4Edge Ltd., Essex

Holy is his name.

And his mercy is on them that fear him from generation to generation.

He hath shewed strength with his arm; he hath scattered the proud in the imagination of their hearts.

He hath put down the mighty from their seats, and exalted them of low degree.

He hath filled the hungry with good things, and the rich he hath sent empty away.

(Luke 1:49-53)

CONTENTS

FOREWORD

Grasp the things of the future
Through the things of the past . . .

Towards the end of 1920 the events of the General Anthroposophical Section were focussed on Rudolf Steiner's dispute with
Oswald Spengler's book, *The Decline of the West*,[1] and the opening of the Goetheanum with the first High-School course (Sep-
tember/October 1920), in the midst of a battle in the print media
over anthroposophy.[2]

A study of the dynamics and drama of 1920 in the unfolding
of the anthroposophical movement acquires even greater explo-
sive power and depth when we take into account the works and
history that had immediately preceded these developments, and
the world situation we find ourselves in *today* in ecological, economic, societal, social, and medical terms. In eight lectures in the
period from the end of October to the end of December 1919,
Steiner discussed the approaching so-called 'incarnation of Ahriman', which he foretold would come in the third millennium
after Christ. This was done at the end of a year that had seen the
failure of the first people's initiative for a threefold social order.
Prior to this, from 1914 to 1918, large parts of Europe as it had
previously existed had been destroyed; eight million people had
lost their lives—and the destructive forces of years of war had a
lasting effect on the life of generations of people, on landscapes,
realms of nature, cities, and also on the total structure of society.
The four Mystery Dramas (1910-1913) were performed for the
first time in the years leading up to the outbreak of war, fully in
the sign of the coming developments.

On 26 September 1920, at the opening of the first Goetheanum,
Rudolf Steiner asked Marie Steiner-von Sivers to recite Hilarius
Gottgetreu's lines from the third Mystery Drama, *Souls' Awakening*,
which he had adapted for the occasion. The lines spoke now,

with regard to the Goetheanum—not of a 'sacred place' as in the Mystery Drama, but of a 'place of aspiration'—and the words, 'full of mysteries', became words sounding with 'seriousness'.[3] The following words of Hilarius are also appropriate in a certain respect to the opening of the Goetheanum in 1920, amid unfavourable economic and sociopolitical post-war conditions, and in the face of hatred from opponents: *'What appears of value to me may fail,/ yet even if all the world despises it,/ and it therefore must collapse in itself,/ nevertheless it was once placed before human souls/ on Earth as something to strive for.'* [4]

As is well known, the history of the Goetheanum in the years following 1920 was problematic. The Society was as brittle as described in the Mystery Dramas—'perforated with ahrimanic holes' is how Steiner is supposed to have described the Anthroposophical Society in 1923[5]—most of the individuals were falling short of their potential and, at the end of 1922, the building was destroyed by fire after a year of increasing 'destructive will' by its enemies.[6] Nevertheless, Steiner, in the circle of his co-workers, founded everything anew in December 1923—the building, the Anthroposophical Society, and its Free High School for Spiritual Science. Right up to his death he was completely committed to their further development. The engagement with Ahriman, a central power of evil, the 'ruler of fear' and 'prince of lies' (Sergei O. Prokofieff [7]), was given great significance from a spiritual perspective, right up to Steiner's last article which was published only after his death, in April 1925 ('Von der Natur zur UnterNatur' (From nature to sub-nature).

*

At the end of 2020, in conjunction with the planned performance of the Mystery Dramas, I had wanted to cover in lecture form at the Goetheanum a number of aspects outlined in the action of the dramas as a whole, and in particular the connection of the Mystery Dramas with the task of the Anthroposophical Society[8] and

about the encounter with Ahriman. However, the events had to
be cancelled in the short term due to the corona crisis, or could
only be partially shown in virtual format. I therefore committed
to writing what I had wanted to speak about, and this is now
before you because it belongs to the thematic context of the developments of 1920 as elaborated above,[9] and because the spiritual
drama outlined there has today, in my opinion, lost none of its
significance—on the contrary.

Peter Selg
General Anthroposophical Section
Ita Wegman Institute
Dornach and Arlesheim, December 2020

Ahriman head (section), Rudolf Steiner. Easter, 1915, wax on wooden board, 12 × 11.8 × 19.3 cm. Taken from Mirela Faldey/David Hornemann v. Laer (editor): Im Spannungsfeld von Weltenkräften *('In the field of tension between cosmic forces') Dornach 2020, page 44.*

1. 'THE INCARNATION OF AHRIMAN'
LECTURES AT THE END OF 1919

'This fact [the incarnation of Ahriman]
is preordained for earth evolution.'[10]

In eight lectures given to members of the Anthroposophical Society in Dornach, Stuttgart, Bern, and Zurich between 27 October and 28 December 1919[11], in the year the initiative towards a threefold social structure had failed, Rudolf Steiner addresses the coming incarnation of Ahriman.

'Before even only a part of the third millennium after Christ has taken its course' Ahriman will take on bodily form, will embody himself in a human being and, so Steiner stresses on 1 November 1919 in Dornach[12], this will be 'in the not-too-distant future'.[13] In lectures touching on this theme, Steiner spoke repeatedly of three world-historic and *once-only* incarnations of superhuman beings—of Lucifer's in the third millennium before Christ, of Christ's at the turn of the eras, and the approaching incarnation of Ahriman. These, according to Steiner, are a matter of 'humanity incarnations' that are played out around the axis of the eras BCE and CE. Lucifer and Ahriman have been operating in the evolution of earthly humanity for much longer periods than this. Lucifer, however, only appeared 'in human form' in the third millennium before Christ in 'eastern Asia'—or, as Steiner stated more specifically, in China—in the biography of an individual who had grown up in a family that served the mysteries.[14] From the age of 40 onwards, this individual permeated the mystery content with the power of intellectual discernment, and thus—as a real incarnation of Lucifer—ushered in a new epoch of development. ('He was the first person able to use the organs of human reason, but only based on the mysteries.'[15]) The luciferic wisdom that was enabled by this radiated out as 'ancient primal wisdom', not only through all the culture of Asia, but even influenced the Hellenic period; indeed, it was even a determining

factor in Greek culture, including its highly developed philosophy. Only Judaism, according to Steiner, in the development of
its own unique forces of conscience and morality, opposed the
luciferic influence which was otherwise dominant everywhere,
even eventually leaving its mark on gnosticism. In this way Lucifer or the luciferic impulse had nevertheless made it possible
for human beings to receive the Christ-impulse in their thinking, feeling, and sensibilities, and thus had a partially beneficial
effect—'into the best of what Lucifer gave to human beings, the
Christ-impulse shone'.[16] 'They [the Gnostics] understood Christ
through what people had absorbed from Lucifer.' Steiner had
spoken on numerous occasions in other lectures about the problematic rejection of worldly and bodily matters, or the one-sid-
edness of gnosticism and, in his lecture in Bern on 4 November
1919, he characterized the four traditional Gospels as the necessary 'counterbalance' to the luciferic influence in gnosticism.[17]
The gnostic movement was nevertheless of great significance
and, from a spiritual-historic point of view, also necessary. The
effects of Lucifer's incarnation, according to Steiner, continued
into the fourth Christian century; after this, Ahriman's influence
became more powerful.

*

The working of Ahriman will intensify until his actual incarnation in the third Christian millennium, until his 'western incarnation'—his incarnation *in the West*—about which Steiner spoke in
his first lecture on this theme on 27 October 1919. Up to the end of
December 1919 the focus of his verbal presentation of this coming world-historic event is never the event itself in any detail, but
rather Ahriman's long preparations on the path towards it, his
'machinations' by which he ushers in the 'triumph of his incarnation'. He creates 'instruments', according to Steiner, 'through
which he prepares what is to come',[18] not least among which are
'certain modes of thinking and conceptualizing', which play into
his hands. 'For, you see, Ahriman prepares for his objective very

well.'[19] What is ideal for him is when 'sleeping' human beings regard his 'machinations' as something good, modern, necessary, and absolutely progressive, as something 'appropriate for human evolution'.[20]

What, in detail, are these preparations and instruments that Steiner spoke about at the end of 1919?

He cites among other things the tendency to elevate an intellectual and rationalistic natural science to absolute and quasi-religious terms, to scientism or, according to Steiner, to the 'superstition' that research based on sensory empiricism is by definition the only path to 'the truth'. Ahriman has the 'very greatest interest' in such a development. In Zurich, on 27 October 1919, Steiner said:

> He would have the greatest success, would experience the strongest triumph, if it could be brought about that the scientific superstition that has taken hold of all circles today, and according to which people even want to arrange their social sciences, were to dominate into the third millennium, and if Ahriman could come to the world as a human being within western civilization and find scientific superstition there.[21]

Among other things, Steiner includes in this 'scientific superstition' that is to become practical reality, the mathematical and mechanical perception and research of the cosmos, whose method postulates the cosmos to be a great 'mechanism', and astrophysics and astrochemistry the *sole* means by which knowledge of 'celestial space' can be acquired. Becoming increasingly widespread and popularized is the notion that 'what surrounds the Earth [...] is devoid of spirit, devoid of soul, and even devoid of life.'[22]

Steiner also spoke about how satisfying economic needs and distracting the populace of the well-to-do industrial nations was a targeted strategy in Ahriman's preparation, by which humanity was to be deluded about its 'most important concerns'. He spoke about the promotion of 'the economist type', who would

become increasingly dominant and in the end would even completely dominate political activity—'*the rulers are merely the
henchmen of economist individuals*'.[23] In the future, everything
other than economic reality would be regarded as no longer rel-
evant, including the world of ideas; universities would then be
dominated by nominalism, 'life in words', and intellectual theo-
ries. Even the knowledge preserved in libraries, that no longer
finds its way into life, is regarded by Steiner in this context as
'good promotional material for Ahriman'.[24] Spiritual impulses
would increasingly be declared chimeras and become cut off
from their potential effectiveness. Distortions of Christology
were also given great importance in this connection by Steiner.
Most especially advantageous for Ahriman's incarnation, however, are materialistic interpretations of the Gospels or the events
at the turning point of the eras. Nowhere would the dominion
of materialism be stronger or more successful than in this area.
Modern theology would become completely alienated from the
cosmic Sun-spirit of Christ and his incarnation, only disseminat-
ing a teaching of 'the simple man of Nazareth', and vilifying all
paths to the spiritual knowledge of Christ as a reality. By this
means the spiritual background of existence, the spiritual history
of the world and of the mystery of the Earth, would be concealed,
including all knowledge of the threefold incarnation configura-
tion of Lucifer, Christ, and Ahriman. As Steiner said repeatedly,
Ahriman's intentions would be promoted '*most of all*' by this 'not
going further' than Jesus, by purely external Christianity. 'The
various confessions are precisely areas, soil, that is advantageous
to the ahrimanic being.'[25] In Zurich, on 27 October 1919, he said:

> For this reason the people who are beginning to form a flock for
> Ahriman when he appears in human form in modern civilization,
> are precisely those who today swear only on the Gospels and, in
> their confessions and sects, dismiss any kind of real spirit-knowl-
> edge, who don't want to learn, who reject everything that requires
> spiritual effort for concrete research and knowledge. Whole
> hordes of followers will emerge for Ahriman from these circles.[26]

In general, according to Steiner, there will be a dramatic increase in people splitting up into opposing groups, and in far more than just religious questions. Militant disagreements over scientific 'evidence' and 'proof' of a pursued project will also intensify more and more. Different groups, Steiner predicted, will claim the indisputability of scientific 'fact' for themselves and their particular view; but 'in all these things one could just as precisely prove the opposite'.[27] The cited 'proof' does not extend to reality or into the 'depths' of existence, it only touches the surface of reality. On 1 November 1919, in connection with this, he said:

> Then they will prove the opposite, one person this, another person that, one group this, another group that; and because it is possible to prove both sides, people will slide into hatred and bitterness, which we certainly find in ample quantity in our time. These again are all things that Ahriman wants to encourage in order to advance his own incarnation on Earth.[28]

Of particular assistance in Ahriman's preparations is the use of numbers, 'statistical proof' and a general belief in the validating power of number, the absolute trust in what is 'objectively' quantifiable. 'And Ahriman does his calculations with the numbers that people believe in [...]. Only afterwards do we see how reliable his numbers are.' 'It is by means of number that people are led astray in a certain direction, through which Ahriman can best find his calculation for his future incarnation in the third millennium.'[29] 'As long as we do not look beyond number to the qualitative element, look beyond number and see the qualitative aspect, we can be deceived the most by number.'[30] Ahriman, according to Steiner, can achieve the most 'when numbers are cited as proof, are seen as evidence'.[31]

*

Ahriman will try by all means and methods to keep anthroposophy in the form of spiritual science out of public life; there is no

greater service one could do for Ahriman than to 'bring it about
that a number of people do not read anthroposophical literature',
said Steiner on 28 December 1919 in Stuttgart.[32] This was shortly
after the papal ban for Catholics against reading theosophical
writings was extended by the Jesuit priest Otto Zimmermann,
in November 1919, to anthroposophy. Targeted public defama-
tions of anthroposophy, according to Steiner, are definitely to be
seen in this connection. Anthroposophical spiritual science *as
such* disturbs Ahriman's preparations for his incarnation, as do
its practical initiatives, which is why the threefold social order is
so strongly opposed. The national unified state, irrespective of
its constitution and structure, is the 'path' towards Ahriman's
incarnation.[33] This is why the basic idea of a threefolding of
society is rejected so aggressively. 'Ignoring the most important
truths' builds for Ahriman the 'best bridges' for his incarnation
to 'thrive'. Here he works with social division of all kinds, not
only national boundaries but with the apparent divisive element
in heredity, the separating off into families, nations, races, etc.
'Everything that can separate groups of people, what keeps them
away from mutual understanding over the whole Earth, what
separates and divides them—this at the same time promotes
Ahriman's impulse.'[34] *'This is here [now], this is operating in present-
day humanity.'*[35]

*

According to Steiner, Ahriman will incarnate in a Western incarnation 'which could then barely be called civilization in the sense
that we understand it'[36] (of which the situation in America in
2020—and for a long time prior to this—gives us an inkling). As
stressed earlier, Steiner does not cite the particular circumstances
of this incarnation in detail, but does make the following remark,
in a lecture in Bern on 4 November 1919:

> Humanity will have to approach the incarnation of Ahriman con-
> sciously amid the convulsions that will take place on the physical

plane. Faced with the continual straits of war and other crises in the near future, the human mind will become very inventive in the sphere of physical life. And through this inventiveness in the sphere of physical life, which cannot be prevented in any way by various action—it will take place as a necessity—through this it will be possible for a human bodily individuality to exist of such a nature that Ahriman will be able to incarnate into it.[37]

In connection with this 'inventiveness' in the 'sphere of physical life' briefly touched on, Steiner also mentions future manipulations of the human body to amplify cognitive functions ('People will learn what they have to eat and drink in order to become extremely clever.'[38]). In the end Ahriman will 'walk' over the Earth with 'immense power with regard to earthly intellectual force'.[39] And this development, the development towards Ahriman's incarnation and intensified activity is, according to Steiner, unstoppable; indeed is a part of the necessary evolutionary history of humanity on Earth—and not a self-caused misfortune: 'This fact [the incarnation of Ahriman] is preordained for earthly evolution.'[40] The important thing, however, is to experience consciously the event of his incarnation and its necessary preparations, to be wide awake and attentive in following all its stages—'what matters is that humanity doesn't sleep through Ahriman's appearance'.[41] According to Steiner we have to see through the ahrimanic 'machinations' and find the right inner relationship to them; a lot will depend on whether Ahriman manages to make all human beings his 'followers', or on the kind of resistance he meets in individuals or communities. What is most pressing therefore is to 'fully recognize' in good time these ahrimanic preparations and forces, and the forces 'through which the ahrimanic element operates'—but also to recognize the forces of resistance through which humanity can arm itself, 'so as not to be tempted and seduced by these ahrimanic powers'.[42] 'We must learn to recognize what is working in the world and respond accordingly for the sake of the world'.[43] Whether we are ready and able to encounter with 'full consciousness' the incarnation of Ahriman and all his preparations, without being able to prevent or avoid it, will, according to Steiner, be a question in the near future of courage, energy, and will. What Steiner considered to be essential here is an intensive, critical and precise examination of contemporary natural science and its materialistic character, which was his life's work. He stressed how important it is not to leave science completely in the hands of Ahriman, not to avoid and bypass it, but rather to engage with it fully and completely—including its partially illusionary dimension—to enter into it fully, albeit with critical awareness. On 2 November 1919, Steiner explained that it was a matter of bringing luciferic forces into the ahrimanic business of science—enthusiasm, warmth, devotion—in order to prepare a path for the effective Christ-impulse—'then by our own luciferic interest we separate from Ahriman something that actually should belong to him [science]'.[44] The broadening, the 'lifting' or imbuing of science with spirit, its permeation by the Christ-impulse, is the goal[45] through which the potential transformation of astrophysics into astrosophy was so exceptionally highly valued by Steiner.[46] 'Spirit and soul' must be sought and found once again in the cosmos—'This is what Ahriman [...], for the success of his incarnation, would most especially like to avoid.'[47]

In the opposite direction it is precisely the ahrimanic forces that need to be employed on the inner path of self-training, i.e. the forces of exact observation and sober analysis in introspection. 'When we go into ourselves with our own ahrimanic aspect' and develop inner objectivity with 'ahrimanic cold-bloodedness'[48] and relentless self-knowledge, we work against the luciferic tendency of our inner soul-life, against the temptation towards self-absorbed esotericism and mysticism, against overestimating our person and its ostensible potentials, and also against erroneous—because egocentric—dealings with anthroposophy.

Further to this subject, Steiner articulated various other possible means by which to resist the coming Ahriman incarnation or already to impede its preparations. Thus he spoke about creating a free intellectual and spiritual life as part of a threefold social order, about understanding the Gospels through spiritual science, and about using the realism of the idea to penetrate into 'the inner nature of things'[49] (instead of the dominant nominalism and subjective constructivism). He left no doubt, however, that the coming developments were unstoppable. The being of Ahriman *will* come, but people can confront him and determine for themselves 'what they might learn from him, what they will accept from him'—*and what they won't.*[50] It will be of decisive importance to face him, Ahriman, 'eye to eye', and take a 'free stance' towards him. It would even be possible in a certain way to make something good out of Ahriman's incarnation. In this connection Steiner said the following on 4 November 1919 in Bern:

> People will have the task in the coming development of civilization to approach Ahriman's incarnation with such fullness of consciousness that this Ahriman incarnation will actually serve humankind by encouraging a higher spiritual development because people become aware, precisely through Ahriman, what the human being can achieve or, let's say, can not achieve, through purely physical life.[51]

Knowledge of and insight into Ahriman will show clearly the boundaries and limited significance of the physical, and therefore also of purely intellectual, unspiritual life. A clear recognition of the ahrimanic—and the luciferic—opens the path to Christ and makes it possible.[52]

im Licht erfahrung

Bewusst ~~wird~~ sein Weltenziel ~~erzeugen~~

füßt er Schmerzen durch das

So ~~will~~ ~~dem~~ Menschendenken, ~~~~

dereinst

In dem er doch ~~~~ Erlösung finden

frei   seiner   zu   schaffen   wird.

Und ~~muss~~ von Qual~~en~~ ~~~~ ~~~~ - -

Versuchte er   die

~~Er wollte~~ ~~~~ Augenblickes Gunst

erst noch   zu nützen

Bei Strader ~~nach~~ in seiner Art ~~erlauschen~~;

Verbergend sich, doch sich auch offenbared.

wird er

~~~~ den Schülern meines Mystenkreises ~~~~

sein Wesen künftig

~~~~ nicht verhüllen können.

sollen   stets

Sie ~~werden~~ ihn in Wachsamkeit ~~~~ denken. — —

in   wallen

Wenn er ~~~~ ihrem Schauen ~~~~ wird,

Dann mögen

~~Sie~~ ~~~~ sie die vielen Formen deuten,

ent   ver   f

Die ihn ~~verhüllend~~ doch ~~enthüllen~~ sollen. - -

Du aber, Straders sonnenreife Seele,

~~Die aber~~ ~~~~

Du wirst als Geistesstern ihr Sein erleuchten,

Dass sie im Innern sich das Licht erkraften,

Und so als geisteslichtes Offenbarer

Gedankenkräftig sich auch dann bezeugen,

Wenn über vollerwachtes Geistesschauen

Der finstre Ahriman, Weisheit ~~~~ lähmend

Des Chaos ~~die~~ Dunkelheit ~~~~ breiten will. — —

ver

~~~~ -

(Vorhang fällt) -

Rudolf Steiner: handwritten corrected typescript, the master copy of the last page of the fourth Mystery Drama. Taken from: GA 44, p. 430.

2. 'The Awakening of Souls'
Ahriman in the Mystery Dramas,
1910-1913

'There is only one region in the land of spirit
In which the sword can be forged
At the sight of which you must vanish.'[53]

In the years between 1910 and 1913, in his *Four Mystery Dramas*, Rudolf Steiner brought to view on the stage in highly dynamic action, what for many years had been the content of his anthroposophical spiritual science. The Dramas have a clearly outlined connection with the development of the Anthroposophical Society[54] and were intended as a means to school the members, and therefore also to impart knowledge to them, even to the point of presenting on stage a study of Ahriman's nature ('...a teaching of his nature...'[55]), and portraying his strategies and activities, which it is important to see through. Johannes Thomasius says at one point about him:

> What people opine to know about him
> Has no value. He can only be understood
> By one who has seen his being in spirit. [56] *

How is Ahriman portrayed in the Mystery plays in his being and mode of operating? What perception of himself is the basis of his action? He speaks of his 'solidity' and the 'hardness' of the 'firm ground' that he makes possible for human beings by orientating their senses and intellect, but also through the densifying, scleroticizing forces that emanate from him. He is the 'knower of cosmic laws', the laws of his own ahrimanic

---

*In this book, quotes from Steiner's *Mystery Dramas* are translated literally. For a more artistic rendering see the translation *Four Mystery Dramas* by Ruth and Hans Pusch, published by SteinerBooks.

earthly world and of the 'cosmos' as understood by physics; he is present in earthly form, can be seen with 'bodily eyes' in all the 'evolutionary progress of the Earth', in the condensed light of sense-perception—and he promises human beings, in their exclusive orientation towards the sense-related intellect, the attainment of 'self-awareness' (I lead you / into true being'[57]). Ahriman is an intelligent tempter, 'father of all illusion', and a 'spirit of deception' who works with aspects of the truth, 'cleverly calculating'. He takes possession of sleeping human souls, but also of their good works to the extent that people are not able to maintain and protect the connection between these and the best forces of their individuality. 'I would then have to love Ahriman / And joyously give into his possession / What arises from me in the realm of earthly life,' Johannes Thomasius says.[58] He is not speaking just about a book, however, but about his entire human being. Ahriman binds people to the Earth and to earthly life, fixes them to what is sensory, physical, and singular. Thus he opposes with such energy in the Dramas the 'crazy knowledge' of reincarnation and any memory relating to it, which he tries to belittle as subjective projection—'That Benedictus merely took images from your own head / Which he transposed into earlier times: / You can find clearly from your own knowledge...'[59] Maria is the first in Benedictus' circle of pupils to freely resist Ahriman on this point. She knows the significance of modern spiritual science—of spiritualized intelligence—for this confrontation, and expresses it explicitly:

> The lofty powers of destiny have wisely
> Appointed you [Ahriman] as the Adversary;
> You benefit everything you wish to hinder.
> You bring the power of freedom to human souls
> When you penetrate into the foundations of their soul.
> From you spring forth the forces of thought
> Which, although they are the illusory images of knowledge,
> Are nevertheless also what leads to a sense of truth.

> There is only one region in the land of spirit
> In which the sword can be forged
> At the sight of which you must vanish.
> It is the realm in which human souls
> Fashion knowledge from forces of intellect
> And then transform it into spirit-wisdom.
> And if, in this moment, I can rightly
> Forge the word of Truth into a sword,
> You will have to leave this place.
> So hear, you who are the father of deception,
> Whether I utter before you the truth of victory. [60]

Maria resists Ahriman with an explicit reference to her memory of an incarnation in the fourteenth century CE, the content of which is closely connected with the destiny-laden circumstances in the development of the new spiritual science ('Memory of that time gives me / Now the strength to oppose you'[61]). Maria evades Ahriman, he cannot conquer her soul—and through her protection of Johannes Thomasius he has no direct access to him either. Both are consciously sent by Benedictus into Ahriman's realm, are sent directly to him supported by the 'Guardian of the Threshold', the great Guide of humanity. 'Where do I find the strength to resist inwardly?' Thomasius asks Maria in the face of Ahriman's proximity.[62] She stands by him:

> My earnest, sacred vow radiates power;
> And your soul can bear the pressure
> If you choose to feel its healing effect. [63]

Ahriman is thus not able to get near to two of the main protagonists in the destiny drama. 'The time is unfavourable for my activity / I find no access to these souls,'—this is how, in the 'Sun-temple' of the second Mystery Drama, Ahriman sums up his situation at that time. [64]

*

Nevertheless, he is powerful. In the third drama, Scene Eight, his own realm is specifically portrayed, his 'realm of death' (Strader). It becomes clear that spiritually-seeking souls— Rosicrucians, in the drama—often receive instruction here because they are not able to recognize his being: 'They see me and do not recognize me.' They are there during sleep and Ahriman can employ them for his own purposes; he can 'count on them' and utilize them. It is of decisive importance for him, however, to win over the main protagonists in Benedictus' community. Strader, the technologist who despite initial doubts finds his way into the spiritual teachings and community, is led by Benedictus into Ahriman's realm in order to encounter him and emancipate Strader's work from Ahriman entirely. 'What spirit stands before my soul?'[65] By his own testimony, Ahriman has command 'where forces that are mechanically useful gain strength from creative sources'.[66] This is why his knowledge is so essential for Strader, who seeks through spiritual knowledge to bring about technological changes in the midst of the material world. He, Strader, represents the significance of the new spiritual science for civilization right down to the sphere of mechanics. Ahriman knows how important it is for him to win Strader. Benedictus, Ahriman's true opponent, does not act directly himself but, as a spiritual teacher, through his pupils. These pupils, by entering on the path of soul-spiritual development—that is, by not only absorbing and affirming the new science of the spirit but by internalizing and applying it practically in their individual ways along the paths of their own soul and in their professional work—can champion spiritual science in various areas of life. If they fail in this work or in themselves, Benedictus, according to Ahriman, would stand alone at his lost post— '...he then / Has to rely on himself and his own foundations. / But people do not like these. / The more truly these can reveal themselves, / The more they are hated on Earth.'[67]

Strader consistently follows a path of thinking, a path of intellectual clarity which becomes increasingly spiritualized. Even the plausibility and truth of reincarnation starts to make sense to him initially through his thinking. From ancient times Strader has borne the fire- and Ego-element of will in his destiny, but also the solitude of the loner, and a particular sensibility towards Christ. He had a Jewish past which, according to Steiner, continued to work with its 'gentleness' and 'kindness' into his present incarnation, and he carried a profound seriousness in his being. He possessed evolved individual forces of conscience, and was as far from Lucifer as can be imagined (as far as Judaism was from luciferic Gnosis). In Scene Ten of the third drama, the following is said to Strader:

> You were obliged to stand on the spirit-place
> That strictly commands all thinking to complete stillness.
> Just as your hand would have to guide the hammer
> Into emptiness, and your own strength
> Could never become aware of itself
> If it never hit against an anvil,
> So thinking could never comprehend itself
> If Ahriman did not oppose it.
> In your life, all thinking led you
> To obstacles, which brought pain
> And difficult doubts to your soul.
> Through them you learnt to know yourself in thinking
> Just as light, only through reflection,
> Can behold itself in its power of radiance.[68]

Strader is aware of Ahriman, and also of the tragic element in his place in the evolution of humanity and the world. He even has compassion for him and has an inkling of his pain 'over many thousands of years', which Ahriman speaks about at one point to Johannes Thomasius. Strader says to Ahriman, 'When I think about you, I can only lament, weep.'[69] It is not Strader's sympathy that Ahriman wants, however, but his soul—and he knows that Strader's work poses a danger for him, and that Strader could distance himself from him because Strader places the thinking of his intellect, which he has thanks to Ahriman, at the service of something higher: 'A human being is striving / To eradicate entirely from his being / The spiritual-mental substance he has received from me.'[70] In the interior of the Earth depicted in Scene Twelve of the fourth drama, Ahriman contemplates how he might still win over Strader ('I need Strader now') in order, in one decisive point, to hold back the comprehensive activity and effectiveness of the community around Benedictus: 'I must harm Benedictus through Strader. / Without Strader he will be unable / To achieve anything further with his other pupils.'[71] Strader has realized for a long time that many of the difficulties involved in the practical implementation of his technological ideas are the expression of an inner conflict with Ahriman. 'Am I equipped for this battle also?' he asks Benedictus, full of doubts. Unlike Thomasius' question to Maria, it is not a question here only of sufficient forces to resist Ahriman, but of a real conflict, a 'battle' with him, which the Michaëlic souls of the new spiritual science must wage against Ahriman. Unlike Thomasius, who is supported by the living Maria, Strader is supported by the deceased Theodora; in a certain way Michaël leads him in Ahriman's realm to Christ, whose light had already shone before his eyes in his medieval incarnation, and which he finds again in and through Theodora.

Ahriman finally decides to lead Strader astray through Strader's own technological inventions. He is to be brought to the bitter realization that his new mechanism is defective, wrong in its 'fundamental concept' or at least full of faults. Through the impression of his own error, through his own 'wrong thinking', he is to lose faith in himself. But Strader is acquainted with abysses, including the abyss of his own existence. In Scene Four of the fourth drama he is strongly prompted by Maria, on the path of his esoteric development, to illumine with a light of his own the demons that rise up on the threshold. Benedictus also says to him at the time: 'Look further still into your abyss.'[72] Strader is on the path of spiritual pupillage and is aware of the consuming doubt in the whole depth of his thinking soul. But right to the end, and despite Ahriman's intervention, he does not succumb to it completely; even up to the hour of his death he overcomes himself and remains true to the task with the utmost loyalty. After he had crossed the threshold, the one who watched over him, Theodora, spoke of Strader's 'high soul' and 'dear soul', and Benedictus speaks of his 'sun-mature soul'. Strader, who after a long period of solitude found his way into the community, but despite the support of Theodora remained solitary there too—solitary also in the world-historic dimension of his consciousness-soul and his necessary engagement with technology and matter—Strader needed love, yet worked tirelessly out of love, out of a love 'that creates many forms in life in order to reveal itself'. In the words of the one who took care of him, 'His last thought was for the work / Which he had dedicated himself to with love. In the same way that people separate from beings whom they love—'so Strader's soul left / The earthly work it loved.'[73]

Strader's path of destiny, in the midst of Michaël's confrontation with Ahriman for the future of human intelligence, becomes increasingly a path of sacrifice in Ahriman's territory—the realm of matter and technology. Strader wants to permeate the realm of mechanics with the moral principle, and in this is ahead of his time. What Ahriman wants is the demonic antithesis of Strader's objectives. At the end of the fourth drama Benedictus expresses a conviction that Strader's sacrifice will be of significance for the further destiny of the community. Strader's 'spirit-star' will

shine towards the friends in the future; he will permeate their
existence with his light.

*

Benedictus becomes increasingly involved in the social destiny of the community, with the paths—and false paths—of
its central members. The blame for the situation where Benedictus is himself temporarily unable to recognize Ahriman
even though he sees him, lies evidently in the 'chaos' in the
community, and not in himself (Who are you [Ahriman], who
in the shadows draws life for himself out of my chaos / In the
circle of souls?'[74]). Benedictus' weakness is only temporary,
a weakness that is not a deficiency but a temporary loss of
sovereignty in a distressed and distressing situation. Benedictus knows that everything depends not only on seeing Ahriman but also on recognizing him, being able to *think* him. The
potential release of Ahriman from his world-historical trag-
edy depends on what happens in the human mind. *'O Man,
know me'*—these are the first words Ahriman speaks in Scene
Four of the first drama. They are a challenge, yet in a certain
way can also be heard as a plea.

    Ahriman mainly stays hidden—he is both visible and invisi-
ble at the same time:

> He tries to confuse human thinking,
> Because he seeks in it the source of his suffering
> Through an ancient corrupted error.
> He does not yet know that he can only find redemption
> In the future when he rediscovers his being
> In the mirror of this thinking.
> Thus he does indeed show himself in human beings, but not
> How he feels himself in truth in his being.[75]

'We have been attempting for some years now in Munich to stage our mystery plays, to give them a form such that energy could flow from this side of our spiritual movement,' Steiner said on 10 May 1914 in Kassel.[76] The Mystery Plays are an existential drama of modern people and were written for a Michaëlic community, not least for their confrontation with Ahriman in an earthly world increasingly determined by him. 'And it is our world...'[77]

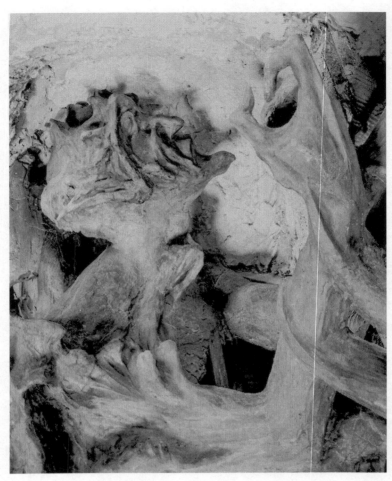

Upper part of Ahriman by Rudolf Steiner, 1916-1917, 1:1 model of 'The Group'. Taken from Mirela Faldey/David Hornemann v. Laer (Ed.): Im Spannungsfeld von Weltenkräften *('In the field of tension between cosmic forces'), Dornach 2020, page 16.*

3. THE BATTLE FOR HUMAN INTELLIGENCE THE LEADING THOUGHTS OF 1924/25, AND THE PRESENT

*'The picture of the human being we consider to be
true, itself becomes a factor of our lives.'*
(Karl Jaspers[78])

*'Confusion and devastation will rule as the year
2000 approaches.'*
(Rudolf Steiner[79])

Right up to his death Rudolf Steiner worked to awaken an awareness of the fact that Ahriman can find his being reflected in the 'mirror' of human thinking, that human beings can know and recognize him, and in a certain respect can redeem him. He saw this realization as being an essential task of the Free High School for Spiritual Science which was to help Michaël enter civilization—Michaël, not Ahriman, even though Ahriman's coming incarnation is 'preordained' for earthly evolution.

At the beginning of the period of Steiner's confinement to his sickbed, in October and November 1924, he still wrote guiding articles about Michaël and Ahriman—about the 'Michaëlic path', about 'Michaël's task in Ahriman's sphere', his 'experiences and ventures in fulfilling his cosmic mission', about 'humanity's future and the activity of Michaël', the 'Michaël-Christ experience in human beings', about 'Michaël's mission in the age of human freedom', and about 'cosmic thoughts in the working of Michaël and the working of Ahriman'. Steiner outlined once more in these articles the spiritual development of humankind as the 'incarnation' of human consciousness 'on the ladder of unfolding thought'. He described the original experiences of thought that were experienced in the Ego and permeated by spirit, soul, and life, that finally descended by way of soul-body and life-body into the physical body, whose sphere of forces they use as a 'mirror' and thereby succumb to advancing abstraction—a process Steiner presented as the price for making personal will and freedom possible. The modern person's Ego is free, or capable of freedom, *because* our thoughts no longer have compelling force or power, but are 'dead shadows', separated off from the existential 'beingness' of the spiritual world from which they originally emerged. The Michaëlic 're-ascent along the lines of the will' is placed squarely in the sphere of human freedom and might remain undone, with the human being becoming a part of the purely physical world, caught up and bound by its pull. Rudolf Steiner described how, up until the beginning of the modern era, ahrimanic intellectuality or spirituality had only slight access to human beings and human intelligence, only 'a quiet hint of power', and how our human being was held by divine-spiritual forces. But then, in the course of the transference of intelligence to human beings who were becoming free, there occurred 'the slide into a different world history' [in which Ahriman plays a decisive part],[80] with great dangers and 'devastating' consequences.

However, Steiner relates at the same time that since the Mystery of Golgotha, human beings can find the Christ-being in Ahriman's sphere, and that Christ, with the assistance of Michaël, can guide them out of it. Christ, whom Michaël himself served, descended from the Sun-realm to Earth 'in order to be there when intelligence becomes fully present in the human individuality'.[81] Through his 'great sacrifice', Christ has been living since Golgotha in the Ahriman-sphere and makes possible for human beings the choice of decision—supported by Michaël who, since the eighth century CE, has followed Christ's path of incarnation to the Earth. According to Steiner, Michaël's cosmic 'gaze' has been directed 'from the beginning' towards humanity—and his goal has always been to maintain a connection between the intelligence that is accessible to humankind and comes to life in it by gradual stages, and divine-spiritual beings. Michaël saw early on the danger of this intelligence becoming alienated and instrumentalized, of its being occupied by ahrimanic beings— 'they want the cosmic intellectuality that they suck in to radiate through the whole new cosmos, and for the human being's continued existence to be in this intellectualized and ahrimanicized cosmos'. [82] Human beings of the present time have to encounter ahrimanic beings and, if they go along with and join them, can either fall to them completely or take the opposite path:

> A researcher of the spiritual world today *is obliged* to make people aware of the spiritual fact that the spiritual rulership of human affairs has passed over to Michaël. Michaël accomplishes what he has to accomplish in such a way that he does not influence human beings by it; but *they* can follow *him* in freedom in order, with the power of Christ, to find their way once more out of the Ahriman-sphere into which they had by necessity to enter. One who can honestly feel at one with anthroposophy from the deepest being of their soul, genuinely understands this Michaël phenomenon. Anthroposophy wishes to be the proclamation of this message of Michaël's mission.[83]

In the age of freedom, Michaël has no compulsive power over free humanity:

> But in the supersensory world immediately bordering the visible one, Michaël can unfold what he wishes to unfold as majestic, exemplary action. In an aura of light, Michaël can show himself there with the gesture of a spirit-being in whom all the splendour and glory of the past intelligence of the gods is revealed.
>
> He can reveal there how the working in the present of this intelligence from the past is truer, more beautiful and more moral than all the intelligence of the present which emanates in deceiving, beguiling glamour from Ahriman. He [Michaël] makes perceptible how *for him* Ahriman will always be the lower spirit under his feet.

Those individuals who supersensibly behold the world bordering the visible world, perceive Michaël and those with him, as
here described, and what they wish to do for human beings. Such
people see how, through the image of Michaël, human beings in
the Ahriman-sphere are to be guided in freedom away from Ahriman to Christ. When people like this manage, through what they
perceive, to open the hearts and minds of others so that there is a
circle of individuals aware of how Michaël lives among us, then
humanity will begin to celebrate Michaël festivals with an appropriate content through which souls will awaken in themselves
the power of Michaël. Michaël will then be active as a real force
among human beings. The human being will be *free* and yet walk
his spirit-life's path through the cosmos in intimate association
with Christ.[84]

In the years before the turn of the twentieth century, in his
engagement with the thought-forms of scientific materialism
and in the sphere of initiation, Rudolf Steiner was himself in
a certain respect also one of those who 'through the image of
Michaël' were guided 'in the Ahriman-sphere... in freedom away
from Ahriman to Christ'. In Weimar in the 1880s he wrote his
Michaëlic *Philosophy of Freedom*,[85] to which he returned explicitly
in his Leading Thought of October 1924:

> To become fully aware of the working of Michaël within the spir-
> itual coherence of the cosmos is to solve the enigma of human
> freedom out of the cosmos itself in so far as this resolution is nec-
> essary for earthly man. [...] In my *Philosophy of Freedom* the 'free-
> dom' of human beings of the present time is demonstrated to be
> a content of consciousness; in the description of the mission of
> Michaël given here, one finds the cosmic basis for the 'coming-in-
> to-being' of this freedom.[86]

In the second half of October and the beginning of November
1924, a few months before his death, Steiner's Leading Thought
articles took on a great and decidedly inward quality. He wrote
of how it is possible and necessary to 'live into' 'what Michaël

and those working with him stand for among us with their deeds and their mission',[87] and about the 'inner perception of Michaël's being and deeds'.[88] Steiner describes in subtle terms the joint working under present conditions of Christ and his 'servant' Michaël in the inner being of the human soul and in its mental-spiritual connection with the outer world. ('Understanding Michaël today means finding the way to the Logos lived by Christ among human beings on the Earth.'[89]) Steiner once described anthroposophy as a 'Christ-Michaël language' that opens up for us the being and evolution of man and the 'coming-into-being of the cosmos', and outlined how Michaëlic cognition and action comprise a spiritual path into external nature that is free of luciferic influences. This path had undoubtedly been taken in an anticipatory way by Goethe in his natural science and world-view—and Goethe's work on, and presentation of, his epistemological methodology was at the centre of Steiner's early books written in Vienna and Weimar.

In the second half of October and beginning of November 1924, however, Steiner also described the inner path to Christ which, since the Mystery of Golgotha, is attainable for the human soul. Christ can be found 'in a fully concrete, humanly deep and clear way' in our inner being, and can lead us to an experience of genuine and true humanity, as well as to a proper stance towards Ahriman ('*Christ gives me my human being*'.[90]) 'Turned spiritually towards the outer world, our gaze on Michaël, and turned spiritually towards the innermost of the soul, our gaze on Christ', we find the god-willed way into the future.[91] It was in this way that Rudolf Steiner himself, at the end of the nineteenth century, advanced to his actual spiritual-scientific and anthroposophical work.

> With regard to external nature, human beings will find the path to the supersensory in the right way through Michaël. A view of nature will be able, without becoming distorted in itself, to stand beside a spiritually accurate view of the world and of the human being as a cosmic being.

Through a proper relationship to Christ, people will be able to experience in living converse with him what it was only otherwise possible to receive as the traditional revelation of faith. It will be possible to experience the inner world of soul as illumined by spirit just as the external world of nature is experienced as held by spirit.

If people were to wish to gain access to their own supersensory being without a close relationship with the Christ-being, this would lead them out of their own reality and into an ahrimanic one. Christ bears within him, in a way that is cosmically justified, the impulse of humanity's future. For the human soul, uniting with him means taking up the seeds of its own future in a cosmically justified way. Other beings, who already show structures that for human beings will only be cosmically justified in the future, are part of the ahrimanic sphere. Uniting with Christ in the right way means safeguarding oneself in the right way against the ahrimanic element.

In those who, in the face of the in-flow of human knowledge, strongly demand the preservation of faith in revelation, there is an unconscious fear that by this means people could become subject to ahrimanic influences. This has to be understood. But it should *also* be understood that it honours and truly recognizes Christ when the flowing-in of the spiritual element by grace into the human soul is ascribed to an experience with Christ.

Thus in future the Michaël-experience and the Christ-experience can stand side by side. The human being will thereby find his proper path of freedom between luciferic aberration into illusions of thought and life, and ahrimanic enticement into future forms that satisfy his hubris but can not yet be *his* present form.

Falling into luciferic illusion means not being fully human, not wanting to advance right to the level of freedom, but wanting to remain at an earlier stage of development—as god-human. Falling for ahrimanic enticements means not wanting to wait until the right cosmic moment for a definite level of humanity, but to anticipate this level too early.

> *Michaël-Christ* will stand in future as the word of guidance
> and orientation at the beginning of the path on which the human
> being, cosmically justified between the luciferic and ahrimanic
> powers, can reach his cosmic goals. [92]

His Leading Thought articles on Michaël, which are an extension
of the karma lectures and are part of the inner, spiritual substance
of the anthroposophical movement, were brought to a culmina-
tion by Steiner in the middle of November 1924. He wrote and
published his article *'Die Weltgedanken im Wirken Michaëls und im
Wirken Ahrimans'* ('Cosmic thoughts in the working of Michaël
and in the working of Ahriman') describing the polarity between
the spiritual powers active in the evolution of the forces of intelligence, and thus also the decisive battle for the (intelligent) human
being in the conditions of the contemporary present and the coming future. Steiner dated the article 16 November 1924:

> Michaël evolved intellectuality throughout the cosmos in the past.
> He did this in the service of the divine-spiritual powers in which
> both he and the human being have their origin. And he will stay
> with this relationship to intellectuality. When this intellectuality
> released itself from divine-spiritual powers in order to find its
> way into the inner being of humans, he resolved to place himself
> from then on in the right way towards humanity, so as to find in
> humanity his relationship to intellectuality. But he wanted to do
> all this in accordance with the divine-spiritual powers, continuing
> as their servant, and by means of the powers with which both he
> and humanity had been connected since their origin. Thus it is his
> intention that intellectuality flow in the future through people's
> hearts, but as the same force as it was when it flowed forth in the
> beginning from the divine-spiritual powers.
>
> With Ahriman the situation is completely different. This being
> separated off long ago from the wave of evolution that belongs
> to the above-mentioned divine-spiritual powers. He positioned
> himself in the far-distant past as an independent cosmic power
> alongside these others. In the present time, although he is indeed

spatially in the world to which humankind belongs, he develops no correlation of forces between himself and the beings that belong rightfully to this world. Only because intellectuality, separated off from the divine-spiritual beings, comes to this world does Ahriman find himself related to this intellectuality to the extent that through it he can connect with humanity in his own way. For he united himself in far-distant primordial times with what people in the present receive as a gift from the cosmos. If he managed to achieve what he intends, Ahriman would make the intellect given to human beings similar to his own.

Now Ahriman acquired intellectuality at a time when he could not internalize it. It remained a force in his being that has nothing to do with heart or soul. Intellectuality radiates from Ahriman as a cold, frosty, soulless cosmic impulse. And those people who are caught up by this impulse develop a logic that appears in a pitiless and loveless way to speak for itself—in truth it is Ahriman speaking in it—in which there is no sign of a proper, inner, heartfelt-soul connection in the person with what they think, say, do.

Michaël, on the other hand, never acquired intellectuality *himself*. He administers it as a divine-spiritual force in which he feels himself connected with the divine-spiritual powers. Through his permeation of intellectuality it is also evident that it is just as possible for intellectuality to be the expression of the heart and soul as it is of the head and mind. For Michaël bears within himself all the original forces of his gods and those of the human being. Thus he does not transmit a cold, frosty, soulless quality to intellectuality, but relates to it in an inwardly warm, soulful way. And herein lies the reason why Michaël sweeps through the cosmos with serious countenance and gesture. Being connected with the contents of intelligence in the way Michaël is, means to fulfil the challenge at the same time of not bringing anything of the nature of subjective arbitrariness, of wish or desire into this content—otherwise logic would be the arbitrary subjectivity of only *one* being rather than an expression of the cosmos. Keeping his being strictly as an expression of cosmic being, making sure that everything stirring internally as his own being remains in this inner being—this is what Michaël regards as *his* virtue. His mind is directed towards the great interconnections of the cosmos—this is what his countenance speaks of; his will, which approaches human beings, is to be a reflection of what he beholds in the cosmos—this is what his bearing and gesture speak of. Michaël is serious in all things, for seriousness as the revelation of a being is the mirror of the cosmos from this being. Smiling is the expression of what flows out from a being into the world.

One of the Imaginations of *Michaël* is also this: He sweeps through the *flow of time*, bearing light from the cosmos as the 'beingness' of his being; forming warmth from the cosmos as the manifester of his own being; in his motions his *being is like a world*, affirming himself only by affirming the world, bringing forces down to the Earth as though from all corners of the cosmos.

By contrast [an imagination] of *Ahriman*: In his operations he would like to conquer space out of time, he has darkness around him into which he sends the rays of his own light. The more he achieves his objectives, the more strongly he has frost around him. He moves as a world that has completely contracted into *one* being—his own—in which he affirms himself only by negating the world. He moves as though carrying about with him the eerie forces of Earth's dark caverns.

When someone searches for freedom without the tendency towards egotism, when freedom for them becomes pure love for an action to be carried out, then they have the possibility of coming close to Michaël; when they want to act in freedom while developing egotism, when for them freedom becomes the *proud* feeling of revealing *themself* in the action, then they are in danger of ending up in Ahriman's territory.

The above-mentioned Imaginations light up out of human love for an action (Michaël), or out of self-love in the action (Ahriman).

By feeling ourselves as a free being in closeness to Michaël we are on the way to bringing the force of intellectuality into our 'whole being'. Although we think with the head, our heart feels the light and dark of thinking; our will rays out our being by having thoughts as intentions streaming into it. The more a person becomes the expression of the world, the more they become a human being. A person finds themself not by searching for themself but by connecting in their will with the world in love.

When, in developing their freedom, a person falls to the enticements of Ahriman, they are drawn into intellectuality as though into a mental automatism in which they are a component and no longer *they themself*. All their thinking becomes an experience of the head; but the head separates it from the life of the heart and the life of the will, and extinguishes its own existence. The human being loses more and more of his essential inner human expression by becoming the expression of his separate existence; he loses himself by *seeking* himself; he withdraws from the world and denies it his love. But the human being only truly experiences *himself* when he loves the world.

From what has been described it is clear that Michaël is the one who guides us to Christ. With all the seriousness of his being, his bearing, his actions, Michaël moves in love through the world. One who holds to Michaël nurtures *love in relation to the external world*. And love must unfold in relation to the outer world initially, otherwise it becomes self-love.

Once this love is present in a Michaëlic cast of mind, *love towards others* will be able to ray back into our own self. This self will be able to love without loving itself. And it is on the paths of a love of this nature that Christ is to be found through the human soul. One who holds to Michaël nurtures love in relation to the external world, and by doing so finds the relationship to the inner world of their soul that brings them together with Christ.

The age that is presently dawning needs humanity to turn its gaze to a world that is experienced as a spiritual world bordering on the physical one, and where such things can be found as the Michaël-being and the Michaël-mission as described here. For the world which people conceive of as nature when looking at the physical world is not the world in which they live directly, but one that is as far *below* the truly human as the Michaëlic element is *above* it. It is just that people do not notice that unconsciously, in forming a picture of their world, actually another one arises. In forming this picture they are in the process of shutting themselves off and falling prey to mental automatism. Human beings can only maintain their humanity if they contrast this picture, in which they lose themselves as though in the picture of their perception of nature, with the other one in which Michaël holds sway, in which Michaël guides the way to Christ.[93]

*

What humanity will have to engage with in the present and near future, requiring an existential exertion of its energies, is outlined by Rudolf Steiner in his last article, completed shortly before his death (on 30 March 1925) and published posthumously in April 1925. In it he describes the 'mechanics of technological events' which since the beginning of the nineteenth century have given the scientific age a new quality, and is in the process of gradually creating an actual 'sub-nature' in which ahrimanic forces work in their pure form. ('By far the greater portion of what operates today through technology, and with which [man's] life is becoming entangled to the highest degree, is *not nature* but *sub-nature*. It is a world that emancipates itself in a downward direction.'[94]) According to Steiner, people must find a relationship to this 'ahrimanic culture', whose scope and influence will continue to grow in the future, in order not to jeopardize their human existence and to be capable of any kind of continuing individual evolution at all. As a pure spiritual science that is and functions as something more and other than a philosophy, it is with these decisive, world-historic circumstances that anthroposophy is engaged. Already ten years prior to this, in January 1915 during the World War, Steiner stressed the following in a lecture in Berlin on Michaël and Ahriman: 'We resist Ahriman by following the path emphasized again and again in our

spiritual-scientific movement: the path of spiritualizing our
human culture, our human capacity for concepts and ideas.'[95]
He continued by saying that through the 'content of a spiritual
science' a 'sense' and 'consciousness' of the reality and activity of
'spiritual forces' must arise anew—by us absorbing the teachings
and by becoming aware through them of our own soul-spiritual
existence, of our active, creative individuality.[96] Then in conclu-
sion, in the final week of March 1925 and at the end of his life on
Earth he wrote:

> People need to find the strength, the inner force of knowledge,
> in order not to be overwhelmed by Ahriman in a technological
> culture. Sub-nature has to be understood as such. This is only pos-
> sible when people ascend at least as far in spiritual knowledge to
> extraterrestrial super-nature as they have descended in technol-
> ogy into sub-nature. This age requires knowledge that goes *beyond*
> nature, because it has to come to terms with the dangerous effects
> of a life-content that has sunk below nature. We are naturally not
> saying here that we should return to earlier cultural conditions,
> but that people need to find how to relate the new cultural condi-
> tions in a proper way to themselves and to the cosmos.
>
> Only the smallest number of people today feel the significance
> of the spiritual tasks emerging for humanity. Electricity, which
> after its discovery was praised as the soul of nature's existence,
> must be recognized in *its* power to divert from nature down to
> sub-nature. But human beings must not slide down with it.
>
> In times when a technology did not yet exist that was inde-
> pendent of nature, human beings found the spirit *in* their view of
> nature. In making itself independent, technology left the human
> being staring at what is mechanical and material and which was
> now becoming the subject of his knowledge. This is devoid of
> any kind of divine-spiritual element connected with the origin
> of human evolution. The purely ahrimanic element rules this
> sphere. Spiritual science creates another sphere, one in which the
> ahrimanic element is completely absent. And it is precisely by
> absorbing with discernment a spirituality to which the ahrimanic

powers have no access that human beings are given the strength to face Ahriman *in the world.* [97]

*

The world in which we have to meet Ahriman today is already showing its unmistakable signature in many things. The rapid destruction of nature, an extinction rate of species that is almost inconceivable in its whole drama and dynamic (with up to 200 species of plant and animal disappearing daily from the Earth), the assault on ecosystems, the zoonotic diseases and pandemics associated with this,[98] and all the consequences of climate change including extremes of weather with heatwaves and droughts, torrential rains and tropical hurricanes, rising sea levels and changing oceanic currents, the melting of glaciers and the polar ice, as well as the thawing of permafrost—all this is a picture of the Earth a brief 100 years after Steiner's Leading Thought article. As never before the Earth is in the hands of Ahriman and gigantic high finance. In 2015, according to Oxfam, the wealth of 62 multi-billionaires was as much as that of half the world's population. In 2014 it had been 80 billionaires in contrast to 3.5 billion others, in 2017 it was reckoned to be only eight.

A study was published in Switzerland in 2020 by the major UBS bank and the professional services firm PwC, according to which the total wealth of the approximately 2200 millionaires increased rapidly worldwide during the Covid-19 pandemic by a total of 10.2 billion dollars. Slightly easier to imagine—not absolutely, but in relative terms—was a report on 10 December 2020 in [the German newspaper] *Die Tageszeitung.* The report quotes research done in America by the Institute for Policy Studies and by a US organization for fair taxation, stating that the wealth of the circa 650 billionaires in the USA increased during the Covid-19 pandemic by a trillion dollars to a total of 4 trillion dollars—so not less than by a quarter. In the midst of the misery of the disease and the misery of the Covid measures, the major digital industry corporations, the operators of large Internet platforms, digital mail-order businesses, and the giant pharmaceutical sector were all making their profits.

At the present time a handful of individuals own trillions while a billion others vegetate on the edge of the bare minimum for survival. According to WHO figures there are 822 million starving people worldwide. Nine million die each year from starvation. The problem is one of fair distribution and food management, of the destruction of huge amounts of food in the rich industrial nations, the industrial and also increasingly the climatic destruction of farm land in the 'Third World'. According to UNICEF, 15,000 children under the age of five die daily of starvation or of avoidable diseases. These are not covered by the mass media, they have no public voice, no influence, no live internet reporting in real time. Jean Ziegler who was UN Special Rapporteur on the Right to Food from 2000 to 2008, estimates around 50 million deaths worldwide as a result of our economic order. The WHO stated that the lockdown measures had caused the next 'terrible global catastrophe'. According to a UN report, circa 1.6 billion people worldwide are threatened with loss of livelihood due to lockdown measures, and 150 million children with acute poverty. While the richest and most powerful people on Earth have accumulated billions in profits during the Corona crisis, famine, unemployment and bankruptcies, as well as medical and psychological problems, have reached extreme proportions. Oxfam reported that up to July 2020 alone, around a further 121 million people were forced into absolute lack of food, and estimates around a million additional deaths from starvation in 2020 as a whole.

But the Covid-19 disease itself, and not just the damage caused by the lockdown measures, affects the poor far more than the rich. Those who are poorer and sicker—low-earners, the unemployed and homeless, with their weakened immune systems— are affected by the pandemic more frequently and more severely worldwide than the well-to-do and those living comfortable lives. But in a vicious circle of true ahrimanic style, the numbers of the poor and sick, the numbers of low-earners, unemployed and homeless are rapidly increasing due to the Corona crisis. 'In the post-pandemic era, the numbers of unemployed, worried, miserable, resentful, sick and hungry will have swelled dramatically'—such was the prophecy in June 2020 of Klaus Schwab, the founder and executive chairman of the powerful World Economic Forum, and Thierry Malleret, senior director of his Global Risk Network. [99]

But it doesn't stop here. In their analysis of the present situation, Schwab and Malleret write of a global 'return of "big" government'[100] in the management of the crisis and its consequences, of an increase in 'governmental control'—also continuing beyond the current Corona measures—a significant increase in the 'role of the state' and its areas of intervention, which they consider to be urgently necessary. They write about a new 'global political order' that must be supervised or co-led by supranational organizations (like the WHO) in a coordinated worldwide battle against the pandemic or against other enemies or threats, including the economic ruin of whole states and their many 'resentful people' due to the causes and consequences of the crises (chapter on 'Social unrest'). 'Today, it is estimated that around 1.8-2 billion people live in fragile states, a number that will certainly increase in the post-pandemic era because fragile countries are particularly vulnerable to an outbreak of Covid-19.'[101] These 'fragile' countries, according to Schwab and Malleret, could become a threat to others through, among other things, a new 'wave of mass migration'[102] which the world community must protect itself against by means, according to the authors, of a new 'global political order' and the comprehensive economic reset of the Earth. They speak of economic damage from the pandemic and lockdown measures of 'monumental proportions' which will generate a 'new world'. There will never be a 'normalization' back to the old and familiar—'the world as we knew it in the early months of 2020 is no more, dissolved in the context of the pandemic'.[103] In July 2020, Schwab and Malleret, two highly influential individuals, were not only expecting further 'waves of infection'[104] but saw a complete 'systemic change' approaching,[105] even though they relativized the purely medical impact of the pandemic—'Unlike certain past epidemics, Covid-19 doesn't pose a new existential threat.'[106] Nevertheless, for many sectors ('like entertainment' [= culture], tourism, the hotel and hospitality industries) there would be no foreseeable return to the *status quo ante*, or rather 'none at all'[107]—also none for the system itself of which these sectors are a part. Yet systemic change has many positive aspects and it is essential to replace 'failed ideas, institutions, processes and rules with new ones better suited to current and future needs'.[108] The 'systemic changes' that began so dramatically were already apparent before the crisis; they were overdue and will now be accelerated—and certainly not only in the area of necessary technologization, automation, digitalization and surveillance. 'It might thus provoke changes that would have seemed inconceivable before the pandemic struck'—monetary policy among them. Schwab and Malleret report 'drastic geopolitical realignments',[109] particularly for 'fragile and failing states'[110], and particularly outline the changes in the final chapter 'Personal reset', liberally sprinkled with positive prognoses. They mention separate, ostensibly slight changes that sound attractive and inviting, which stress inner values and deal with overcoming egotism, but which are possibly Lucifer's influence and contribution to the book as a whole, or aspects of his cooperation with Ahriman in a 'joint venture'. ('Thus, we have no choice but to summon up the better angels of our nature.'[111]) 'Might the pandemic give birth to better selves and to a better world? Will it be followed by a shift of values?'[112] According to Schwab and Malleret, it is about 'Redefining our humanness,' about 'Mental health and well-being', about 'Changing priorities'[113]—apparently primarily for members of the leading industrial nations who order books like *The Great Reset* from Amazon, and read them. For Klaus Schwab, already on 3 March 2020, the

Corona crisis was a 'rare but narrow window to reflect, re-imagine and reset our world'[114]—a point of view which in the summer of 2020 he re-emphasized and elaborated on, quoting himself.[115]

*

The elites of the leading industrial nations had evidently been aware for some time of the dangerous instability in the ahrimanic alignment of their neo-liberal systems, including 'transformational' crises of the most varied kinds, provenance and orientation. According to well-documented studies, the scenario of a global 'lockdown' due to a viral pandemic—with interventions in ecological systems as a result—was tested in all its details more than 20 years ago in the crisis planning of elite US groups. Paul Schreyer describes how at the end of the 1990s at John Hopkins University, a centre was set up, financed by billionaires and other private donors, for 'biodefence', or later 'biosecurity', and finally for 'health security', in cooperation with powerful military-industrial and health-political organizations as 'a fulcrum of scientific conferences, emergency exercises and, above all, the continued dissemination of fear-evoking themes among the public. This is where researchers, military personnel and politicians came together, where plans and guidelines were worked out which soon had a defining influence worldwide.'[116] The participants worked on the challenges of biological weapons and plagues in, according to Schreyer, 'an inscrutable grey zone of defending against dangers, and creating them'.[117] The meetings centred on planning for pandemics and, initially, on essential crisis management in the event of a biological weapons attack (later of a 'natural pandemic'), and took the form of simulation games or exercise scenarios designed to create fear in the populace so as to gain political room to manoeuvre; but anxiety and fear are the core tools of Ahriman's activity. The centre's first conference took place in 1999 in a luxury Washington hotel not far from the Pentagon, with more than 900 participants from 10 countries,

including military personnel, politicians, bureaucrats, researchers, representatives of lobbying organizations and leading pharmaceutical companies. For two days they considered the question of biological terrorism. New pharmaceutical products 'in
the interests of national security' played a central role right from
the start and were given the highest priority. Richard Clarke,
National Coordinator for Security, Infrastructure Protection, and
Counter-terrorism for the United States, emphasized at the time:

> For the first time the Deparment of Health and Human Services
> is part of the national security apparatus of the United States. ...
> The current bioterrorism initiative includes a new concept: the
> first-ever procurement of specialized medicines for a national
> civilian protection stockpile. As new vaccines and medicines are
> developed, that program can be expanded. The initiative includes
> invigoration of research and development in the science of bio-
> defense; it invests in pathogen genome sequencing, new vac-
> cine research, new therapeutics research, and development of
> improved detection and diagnostic systems.[118]

These proceedings were certainly not only in political hands,
however; they were developed with substantial input from the
large health-industry corporations as 'global, industrial pandemic management' (Hardtmuth[119]) that could be implemented
or rolled out by overwhelmed governments in situations of
national emergency. Already in 1999 there was discussion on
how, in situations of threat, to develop a targeted strategy
to use the media to convey a consistent and coherent message
to the public—and how to circumvent the presence of unofficial
channels that did not broadcast the desired version of the threat.
('The participants discussed how to control the message going
out to the public.'[120]) The information presented by the media
had to be 'coherent and credible' in order to achieve or compel
the broadest possible consensus in the population on the necessity for vaccinations. Discussions went on all day about emergency powers for the authorities, the suspension of parliaments

and basic rights, and many related questions—'How far can the police go to keep patients in quarantine?' 'Without vaccines, the only method of control is isolation, which hinders the spread of the disease but is not sustainable.' [121]

At a press conference on 27 February 2020 the German health minister, Jens Spahn, reported that at the end of 2019 plans were already being made in the German Ministry of Health to establish a new department for 'Health security' (i.e. *biosecurity*), under the leadership of a uniformed general of the Federal armed forces. 'We decided two or three months ago that there would be a new department in the Federal Ministry of Health, a department for health security, because over the past few years we have noticed that this subject—how to prepare for situations such as this and how we are interconnected in Europe and internationally—has gained ever greater significance.'[122] The uniformed general (!) responsible for this department in the Ministry of Health had previously been in charge of a Nato office for 'early diagnosis of infectious disease outbreak close to real time', and with a 'centralized monitoring of deployed forces'.[123] The US concept of 'biosecurity', which brings together the interests of the military and the medical-pharmaceutical industries, thus gained institutional entry into the German Ministry of Health.

The pandemic scenario played out in 1999 was already about the outbreak of a worldwide epidemic plague. The large sums of money that were invested at the time and in the following years up to 2020 to establish the 'biosecurity' or 'health security' structures and their plans of action, at no time served to *prevent* zoonotic diseases and pandemics which the ahrimanic economic system and its forms of dominance helped to cause and accepted; at no time did they serve as a prophylaxis or a means of fighting the causes, but rather as a system-conformist yet at the same time a system-transformational management that in addition was to be a lucrative business for large individual corporations.

*

As stressed above, these profiteers included, among others, the driving forces for the complete digitalization of the Earth. According to Schwab and Malleret:[124] 'With the pandemic, the "digital transformation" that so many analysts have been referring to for years ... has found its catalyst.'[125] This interests Ahriman or he actually directs it. His concern is not only digitalization but also the comprehensive capture in digital form of all information concerning humanity, including all biometric and health data. During Corona this has not only been propelled forward towards the goal but, in the conditions and progress of the pandemic danger, is increasingly approved by society. This vision of the total digital acquisition of the world's population has already existed for many years in leading corporate and political circles—for the purposes of population and development planning and management, and also with regard to the long-lamented 'overpopulation' of the world which is to be 'regulated' (not, as is known, only for 'humanitarian' and ecological reasons but because the many young people in impoverished countries pose a potential threat to the existing power structures). Ahriman's objective of the comprehensive capture in digital form of all human souls and bodies on Earth, their 'digital identity', requires the biometric capture of every individual, their immunization and other data, right into their molecular structure, and was planned and already set in motion some time ago with the aim of creating a universal health information system. Even the way the new science is expressed linguistically as 'epidemonomics' (Timothy Grant Evans), which contains the word 'demon', has existed for some time.[126] At the Davos World Economic Forum—led by Schwab and financed by the Rockefeller Foundation, Microsoft, and the 'immunization alliance' established by the Gates Foundation consisting of pharmaceutical concerns, governments, the World Bank and the WHO—a trial model was presented in January 2020 which by the beginning of 2020 had been able to acquire the digital biometric data of over 100 million people in Bangladesh and connect this with other information including their vaccination status ('ID 2020'). The goal of this is clearly the complete digital capture of 'world citizens', the central storage of their data in giant US corporations with leading cloud services (like Amazon and Microsoft). This would go hand-in-hand with the abolition of cash: bank-account transactions would only be permitted in future on presentation of a digital ID, thereby perfecting the means of surveillance and control.

In a highly technologized country like China, developments of this kind are already well known to be far advanced. In his book, *Realitätsschock* (Reality shock), Sascha Lobo writes about 'the ditgitally empowered authoritarianism' of the China model which he regards as a potential 'export hit' in the area of Western democracies—a 'combination of dictatorship and economic boom made possible by a radical digital orientation in the economy, without regard to loss of basic rights'[127]—chapter title: *'Das chinesiche Jahrhundert beginnt'* (The Chinese century begins). In 2020, China—and also Hong Kong and South Korea—became the model state for the fight against Corona, with a 'secure lockdown', and the electronic surveillance of sources of danger and people posing a hazard, with 'digital tracing' and surveillance of individuals through their mobile and credit card data, a surveillance that has to function seamlessly and thus cannot be based on individual free will, as Schwab and Malleret stress: 'No voluntary contact-tracing app will work if people are unwilling to provide their own personal data to the governmental agency that monitors the system; if any individual refuses to download the app (and therefore to withhold information about a possible infection, movements and contacts), everyone will be adversely affected.'[128] It is a matter of agreeing on 'a unified model of digital tracing'[129], and, beginning with the current pandemic and with a view to future ones, of heralding in an era of 'active health surveillance made possible by location-detecting smartphones, facial-recognition cameras and other technologies that identify sources of infection and track the spread of a disease in quasi real time'[130]. Even beyond the current infection and with a view to a system and lifestyle change, Schwab and Malleret advocate 'online' and 'telemedicine', and wearable and at-home 'diagnostic tools' such as 'smart toilets capable of tracking health data and performing health analyses'.[131] According to their prognosis, three sectors will flourish and expand after the pandemic with the help of digital technology and 'artificial intelligence' (AI): 'big tech, health and wellbeing'.[132]

> The combination of AI, the IoT and sensors and wearable technology will produce new insights into personal well-being. They will monitor how we are and feel, and will progressively blur the boundaries between public healthcare systems and personalized health creation systems—a distinction that will eventually break down. Streams of data in many separate domains ranging from our environments to our personal conditions will give us much greater control over our own health and well-being.[133]

According to the Schwab/Malleret prognosis for the middle of 2020, this 'active health surveillance'—with less of the 'wellness'—will also be introduced in the near future into the industrial sector; the control mechanisms established during the Corona crisis will be preserved and developed:

> As the coronavirus crisis recedes and people start returning to the workplace, the corporate move will be towards greater surveillance; for better or for worse, companies will be watching and sometimes recording what their workforce does. The trend could take many different forms, from measuring body temperatures with thermal cameras to monitoring via an app how employees comply with social distancing. This is bound to raise profound regulatory and privacy issues, which many companies will reject by arguing that, unless they increase digital surveillance, they won't be able to reopen and function without risking new infections (and being, in some cases, liable). They will cite health and safety as justification for increased surveillance.[134]

As reported in a representative survey in spring 2020, China's popularity in Germany was now equal to America's. 'No country in the world has promoted first globalization, then digitalization, and now AI as aggressively and successfully,' Lobo wrote in 2019 [135] and outlined in detail the vision pursued by China of a 'cybernetic society'. 'The principle of current cybernetic ideologies is to constantly monitor society, to recognize patterns in the gathered data, and based on this to direct behaviour.' [136] It is much more than simply a case of suppressing political opposition. All behaviour—including thoughts—is to be gathered, gauged and evaluated to enable the controlling of society. In 2019, before the global virus crisis, Lobo delineated these tendencies in Western industrial countries for economic and 'security-related' interests:

> For some years in two provinces in Canada there has been a system called RTD (Risk-driven Tracking Database). Data are compiled from the police, the health authorities, youth welfare offices and other sources, including estimates of psychological illness, drug abuse and 'anti-social behaviour'. In this way scenarios are calculated for whole neighbourhoods, but also for separate families and individuals. [137]

Society in Europe is also becoming 'an increasingly monitored space'—and this with the agreement of the populace. 'A representative survey in Berlin in the spring of 2018 reported that 75 per cent of Berliners wanted *more* video surveillance...' [138] And: 'The fact that, in matters of surveillance and society monitoring, European countries have not worked as far or as radically as China has more to do with the poorer technology, the opposition of civil society, and the social-liberal influence in politics, than with any lack of desire in the authorities. The erosion of basic rights follows the technological possibilities somewhat more slowly in the West [...]' (Lobo [139])

In his article on 'The world after coronavirus' in the *Financial Times* in March 2020, the historian Yuval Noah Harari warned (as noted by Schwab and Malleret[140]) against an aggressively expanding 'surveillance technology' in the course of the Corona crisis:

> Surveillance technology is developing at breakneck speed, and what seemed science-fiction 10 years ago is today old news. As

a thought experiment, consider a hypothetical government that demands that every citizen wears a biometric bracelet that monitors body temperature and heart-rate 24 hours a day. The resulting data is hoarded and analysed by government algorithms. The algorithms will know that you are sick even before you know it, and they will also know where you have been, and who you have met. The chains of infection could be drastically shortened, and even cut altogether. Such a system could arguably stop the epidemic in its tracks within days. Sounds wonderful, right? The downside is, of course, that this would give legitimacy to a terrifying new surveillance system. If you know, for example, that I clicked on a Fox News link rather than a CNN link, that can teach you something about my political views and perhaps even my personality. But if you can monitor what happens to my body temperature, blood pressure and heart-rate as I watch the video clip, you can learn what makes me laugh, what makes me cry, and what makes me really, really angry. It is crucial to remember that anger, joy, boredom and love are biological phenomena just like fever and a cough. The same technology that identifies coughs could also identify laughs. If corporations and governments start harvesting our biometric data en masse, they can get to know us far better than we know ourselves, and they can then not just predict our feelings but also manipulate our feelings and sell us anything they want—be it a product or a politician. Biometric monitoring would make Cambridge Analytica's data hacking tactics look like something from the Stone Age. Imagine North Korea in 2030, when every citizen has to wear a biometric bracelet 24 hours a day. If you listen to a speech by the Great Leader and the bracelet picks up the tell-tale signs of anger, you are done for.[141]

*

'*The picture of the human being that we hold to be true becomes itself a factor of our lives.*' This is what Karl Jaspers stresses, and it is Ahriman's picture of the human being that in large part is

decisive in the visions of the future we have just looked at—
and not the picture of ethical individualism, of the individuality who shapes society, is socially oriented, self-responsible, free
and mature. Yuval Noah Harari encapsulates this direction once
more: 'People will no longer regard themselves as autonomous
beings who follow their own wishes according to their life, but
rather as a collection of biochemical mechanisms that are constantly monitored and directed by a network of electronic algorithms.'[142] In a certain sense this seems to Harari to be logical
and consistent in so far as it is all based on a materialistic anthropology—an ahrimanic anthropology in Ahriman's handwrit-
ing—for then the following applies: 'Humans, giraffes, viruses
are all algorithms. They differ from computers in so far as they
are biochemical algorithms which have evolved at the caprice of
natural selection over millennia.'[143] 'The individual authentic self
is no more real than the immortal Christian soul, Santa Claus,
or the Easter bunny.'[144] The materialistic ahrimanic notion of the
unfree human being—as an 'assemblage of biochemical mechanisms constantly monitored and directed by a network of electronic algorithms' ('for, you see, Ahriman prepares well for his
objectives'[145])—and the creation of the technology for an unfree
world, are closely connected, indeed inseparable. What Ahriman
wants is for people to support this new world as the 'healthiest',
the 'safest', the most modern, efficient and rational, to see it as
'the best of all worlds'. It is a world that gives them the technological prospect of their own permanent 'optimization' (and possibly of their 'immortality'), not only by using gene-technology
treatments to boost their immune system to fend off external
threats, but also by 'enhancement' in the area of mental capacities and performance, in their bodily appearance and fitness,
in their desired reproduction (its timing and mode), and in
anti-ageing processes. Viewed as analogous to a technical system, the human being is to be technologically improved, even
perfected—'with bodies improved by optimized genomes and
external technology, people can be more beautiful [...], more

intelligent, physically more skilful, socially more integrated, and in general healthier and happier all-round'—according to the programme.[146] Also envisaged is the direct transmission of software into the human brain ('The vision is that in the distant future it will be possible via a chip to download capacities from an app store, such as the moves of a martial sport, or a new foreign language'[147]) and vice versa. This is supposed to take place through a 'neuralink system' (mind uploading), to the point of 'digital immortality' where the content of a human brain is copied onto other 'hardware', and thus the 'software' continues to exist. Already in November 1920 Rudolf Steiner spoke in Stuttgart about the 'purely ahrimanic ideal' that would one day come 'in the West' which consisted of human 'neural vibrations' being 'transposed' to a machine as a concrete 'joining of the mechanical-material principle with the spiritual'.[148]

What many people at present still see as the futuristic 'transhuman' or 'posthuman' fantasies of manic technicians has in fact been under development for a long time, financed by billionaires. In spring 2020 the jet-free night skies during the Corona crisis gave an optimal view of a number of the currently 400 satellites of the Canadian multi-billionaire Elon Musk. Musk and his Space X company are planning soon to send 40,000 private satellites into orbit around the Earth to maximize broadband provision for the Internet, and *perhaps* for other purposes too. A hundred years after Steiner's lectures on the coming incarnation of Ahriman, 'the surroundings of the Earth' are indeed extensively 'devoid of spirit, devoid of soul, even devoid of life', at least in people's consciousness. Musk's Neuralink Corporation for the interconnecting and final fusing of the human brain with machines, founded four years ago, is presently working outside the public eye (unlike his satellites, also unlike his electric car company Tesla and the electronic online payment system Paypal he co-founded). *'Spirits must break worlds/ If what your times create/ Is not to bring desolation and death / To the eternities.'* [149]

*

In November 2019, at the end of the Foreword to his book *Vertei-digung des Menschen* ('In defence of the human being'), Thomas Fuchs wrote:

> Humanism from an ethical point of view is just as much about [...] resisting the dominance of technocratic systems and practical constraints as it is of the self-reification and technologizing of the human being. If we view ourselves as an object, whether as an algorithm or an apparatus determined by neurons, we expose ourselves to the dominance of those who seek to manipulate the apparatuses and control them by socio-technological means. 'For the power of the individual to make of himself what he wants means [...] the power of the few to make out of others what they want.' [Lewis][150]

Since Steiner's Mystery Dramas (1910-1913), Ahriman has undoubtedly continued to write his impressive story of success, with cold intelligence, precision and breathtaking speed in the real 'destruction stream of time'. Together with Lucifer he has already moved large portions of humanity into the virtual world, even made them feel at home there. The question of what is genuine and true, what can be personally experienced and is authentic, is becoming increasingly more complicated in a world of almost perfect simulation, in which the 'appearance of things' can not only precede their reality, but replace this reality altogether. 'It is already possible that the nice online partner or the empathetic online therapist is in reality only a chatbot. And the first health-care robots for dementia patients are already being trialled,' writes Fuchs.[151] At the present time artificial systems can already replace experiences of real relationship: 'When a comfort robot called "Smart Toy Monkey" is supposed to serve as a friend for small children and promote "social and emotional development"; when friendly health-care robots replace human care for dementia sufferers and supposedly listen to their stories; or when psychotherapies follow programmed online treatments that do away with the need to visit the therapist—then machines will become "relational artefacts", as Sherry Turkle terms it.' [Fuchs [152]]

*

This process, intended and given initiative by Ahriman, of replacing people with automata or with technologies based on 'artificial intelligence', has already been in operation for a long time in the workplace. Through the Corona virus, however, as Schwab and Malleret describe, it has gained an unforeseen boost:

> The covid-19 crisis, and its accompanying measures of social distancing, has suddenly accelerated this process of innovation and technological change. Chatbots, which often use the same voice recognition technology behind Amazon's Alexa, and other software that can replace tasks normally performed by human employees, are being rapidly introduced. These innovations pro-voked by necessity (i.e. sanitary measures) will soon result in hundreds of thousands, and potentially millions, of job losses. As consumers may prefer automated services to face-to-face interac-tions for some time to come, what is currently happening with call centres will inevitably occur in other sectors as well.[153]

Schwab and Malleret regret the job losses but see them as inev-itable in the context of 'system change'. They visualize 'online work', 'online shopping', 'online medicine', 'online entertain-ment', 'online education'—indeed the Corona pandemic could become[154] a veritable 'boon for online education'[155].

In the 330 pages of their comprehensive book, Schwab and Malleret fail to mention the situation of children who in many places have lost their school and school community, their daily and social rhythm. Perhaps these are included in the 'boon for online education'. Children do not play a central part in Ahri-man's calculations, computations and vision; the 'personal reset', the new definition of 'our humanity', of our 'mental health' and 'our well-being' is alluding to the capable flexible adult, eager for change, of the leading industrial nations who accepts, favours and supports the rapidly changing world of 'online work', 'online shopping', 'online medicine', and 'online entertainment' from the centre of his home office (which was already described in Rudolf Steiner's Mystery Dramas: *The energies of technology will be so distributed / That every person can comfortably use / What he needs for his work / In his own home, which he arranges according to his own tastes.*'[156]).

We read nothing in Schwab and Malleret about children or social communities, nor about the fractures in people's network of relationships caused by having no alternative but the 'home office' and the transition into the substitute world of virtual space. Nor do we read about the fractures arising from the very different individual views and reactions to the crisis, to the pandemic and the measures against it, which have led to mutual lack of understanding, loss of trust, and the end of friendships[157]—all likewise very much part of Ahriman's intention and strategy. All this amidst a decidedly pugnacious mass media in certain quarters, working at a highly emotional level, that pillories any questioning, interpretation or behaviour that deviates from the norm, pours scorn, malice and hatred over it, categorizes critical individuals and condemns them. *'Where are the ahrimanic forces? They are there where forces separating people can intervene,'* wrote Rudolf Steiner in his notebook in November 1920.[158]

If, with this background of the times, we remember Steiner's Mystery Dramas, his extraordinarily differentiated lectures and writings on Ahriman and Ahriman's coming incarnation as a human being, his many words of warning—we might think of Hilarius' speech in the last Drama: *'I have often heard them; but only now / Do I feel the secret they contain.'*[159]

*

In our contemporary times the 'secret' contained in Steiner's descriptions concerning Ahriman is becoming more and more evident. The civilizational phenomena of ahrimanic intelligence and its global power, and 'surveillance capitalism' (Snowdon), are increasing at breakneck speed, the 'suppression' of individual thinking that Steiner warned us about ('...that all individual thought will be shut down'[160])—one doesn't have to be 'clairvoyant' to be able to see all this clearly. 'It doesn't help to have illusions about these things,' said Steiner on 27 October 1919 with regard to these Ahriman-dimensions, more than a hundred years ago.[161] And in Dornach a few years later he stressed that anyone who still did not believe that 'things are this serious' was only promoting Ahriman's incarnation.[162] In Scene Eight of *The Guardian of the Threshold* (1912), Ahriman still says: 'Up to now I have had no success in this,/ The Earth did not want to surrender to me,/ But I will strive through the eternities/ Until, perhaps, I gain the victory.'[163] At the end of 2020, this 'perhaps' has become a lot more likely.

As indicated at the beginning of this book, Rudolf Steiner spoke about the unstoppable coming incarnation of Ahriman; but he also spoke about the necessary and possible resistance that could ensure that the Earth and its population did not fall to Ahriman completely. If this fall were to occur, it would mean the loss of 'the Earth's goal' and the real destruction of everything that had hitherto been achieved as 'earthly culture': 'Everything would come about which, as an unconscious tendency, is actually the awful wish of modern humanity.'[164] Rudolf Steiner did describe the possible demise of civilization—a demise that was possible but by no means necessary or inevitable. He was relying in this crisis situation on Michaëlic communities, including the Anthroposophical Society and its Free High School for Spiritual Science, on its knowledge of Ahriman and its counter-initiatives in many areas of life, from education to farming. 'They ought also to think of him [Ahriman] in his watchfulness,/ When he will hold sway in their perception.—/ They must identify the many forms / That conceal him ...'[165] Here—also here—in exceptionally serious times, Rudolf Steiner was building on the potential *community* of Michaël pupils, and was clearly doing so far beyond the existing circle of anthroposophists. There are many 'Michaëlites' in completely other contexts; these are independent and creative individuals with initiative and courage who are active for the future of the Earth, for a new attitude and a new way of treating creation, for ecology and peace. The spiritual tendency of their work is that of the Franciscans or of spiritual Rosicrucianism,[166] although mostly they do not belong to these groups. In the words of Bellicosus: '*The signs of the time clearly show / That all paths should unite.*'[167]

There stands before humanity the unmistakable task of 'saving earthly culture for Christ'.[168.] At the present time the chances of achieving this goal do not seem very great. On the other hand, an 'awakening of souls' is taking place in many places in the world in the face of years of ever-intensifying crises. Fourteen years ago, in his comprehensive and important book *The Ascent of Humanity*, the forward thinking Charles Eisenstein wrote about 'the great crisis of our civilization and the birth of a new age'. Eisenstein's ideas and intentions express what a growing number of people on the Earth are feeling, people whose paths should 'unite'. The 'resistance' Steiner has in mind is not to be equated with denial and rejection; rather, it begins with an effort of human consciousness and a changed and broadened science that serves life, that leads to the creation of models and measures for a life in the various fields of civilization that thrives, as Steiner elaborated convincingly in his dispute with Oswald Spengler and in his *Untergang des Abendlands* ('Fall of the West') in 1920.[169] '*The future of the Earth must be the human being's own design, the human being's own concern.*'[170] In the encounter with Ahriman, with his preparatory 'machinations' and his incarnation, what is needed is a matter of human consciousness—but also a matter of courage, energy, and will. 'Human evolution needs the spiritual, the consciously spiritual impulse for life.' (Dornach, 6 August 1921[171])

If ways are looked for, found and followed, higher help can come. 'Victory', 'which obtains existence out of Nothing through sheer defiance',[172] is mentioned in the Mystery Dramas at a point that also speaks of a plea for help from the spiritual world, a plea for the gracious inclining of the cosmic powers so that our being's light of cosmic spirits may preserve our 'soul's sensing' (*Seelensinn*), our spiritual 'hearing', and the willingness to make sacrifices, which, as with Strader, must be developed individually but can find support from the world of spirit. '*Today, as we prepare in all earnestness to think and feel anthroposophically, we are not standing before small decisions, but before great ones,*'—said Rudolf Steiner on 21 November 1919 in his lectures on the coming incarnation of Ahriman.[173]

There is much to indicate that by a long way not everything is lost, and that—after some profound upheavals—other times and new orders of society, the economy and ecology can come through the action of people and the aid of the spiritual world. The Advent epistle of the Christian Community speaks of the 'image of human becoming which contains divine becoming'.[174] Steiner stressed, on 16 October 1918 in Zurich, that 'unconsciousness' (*Ohnmacht*) and the 'resurrection from unconsciousness' is connected with the Christ Mystery and a modern relationship to Christ Jesus.[175] It is not only the incarnation of Ahriman that is approaching but also the Second Coming of Christ, in the etheric. This can only be met by one who has known unconsciousness, but also the resurrection from it, the real life-principle of the etheric in the overcoming of gravity and the physical decline of 'the dying Earth-existence'. In his long poem 'Wende-Zeit-Spruch' (Verse at the time of change)— in chapter 'Werde wachend' (become awake) of his book *Die Ewige Stadt* (the eternal city)—Friedrich Doldinger begins with the line: 'The time of change has come! / All our protecting huts and shelters are quaking./ And whoever will not grow, / will be shattered by the weight of destinies./ To walk through this horror / is only possible for one who is awake,/ who inwardly receives/ what is coming / with all their strength and humility.'[176]

The ancient words of the Gospel according to St Luke, known for nearly two millennia, indicate that it is still possible to return

all humanity—and not just separate individuals—with the help
of the spiritual world:

> Holy is his name.
> And his mercy is on them that fear him from generation to generation.
> He hath shewed strength with his arm;
> he hath scattered the proud in the imagination of their hearts.
> He hath put down the mighty from their seats,
> and exalted them of low degree.
> He hath filled the hungry with good things;
> and the rich he hath sent empty away.

(Luke 1: 49-53)

NOTES

1   See Peter Selg: *Der Untergan des Abenlands? Rudolf Steiners Ausein-andersetzung mit Oswald Spengler* ('The decline of the West? Rudolf Steiner's dispute with Oswald Spengler'). Arlesheim and Dornach 2020.

2   See Peter Selg: *Die Eröffnung des Goetheanum und die Diffamierung der Anthroposophie* ('The opening of the Goetheanum and the defamation of anthroposophy'). Arlesheim and Dornach 2021 (in preparation).

3   See Rudolf Steiner: *Four Mystery Dramas*, GA 14, and also *Mantrische Sprüche. Seelenübungen, Volume II 1903-1925*, GA 268. Dornach 1999, page 255. (English edition: *Mantric Sayings, Meditations 1903 - 1925 Soul Exercises, 1903-1925*, SteinerBooks 2015.)

4   Rudolf Steiner: *Vier Mysteriendramen (Four Mystery Dramas)*. GA 14. Dornach 1999, page 408.

5   Rudolf Steiner: *Das Schicksalsjahr 1923 in der Geschichte der Anthroposophischen Gesellschaft. Vom Goeanumbrand zur Weihnachtstagung.* GA 259. Dornach 1991, page 302. ('The Year of Destiny 1923 in the History of the Anthroposophical Society').

6   Peter Selg: *Rudolf Steiner 1861-1925. Lebens- und Werkgeschichte. Band 6: Die Zerstörung des Ersten Goetheanum und das Jahr 1923.* Arlesheim 2017. (English edition: *Rudolf Steiner, Life and Work, Vol. 6, 1923, The Burning of the Goetheanum*, SteinerBooks 2018.)

7   Sergei O Prokofieff: *Rudolf Steiner, Fragment of a Spiritual Biography.* Temple Lodge Publishing, Sussex 2020.

8   See Peter Selg: *Esoterische Gemeinschaften in Rudolf Steiners Mysteriendramen* ('Esoteric communities in Rudolf Steiner's Mystery Dramas'). Arlesheim 2010.

9   See notes 1 and 2.

10 Rudolf Steiner: *Weltsilvester und Neujahrsgedanken.* GA 195. Dornach 2006, page 53. (English edition: *Cosmic New Year*, Percy Lund Humphries & Co., 1932.)

11 See Rudolf Steiner: *Soziales Verständnis aus geisteswissenschaftlicher Erkenntnis. Die geistigen Hintergründe der sozialen Frage, Volume III.* GA 191 (English edition: *Understanding Society Through Spiritual Scientific Knowledge*, Rudolf Steiner Press 2017); *Der innere*

Aspekt des sozialen Rätsels. Luziferische Vergangenheit und ahrimanische Zukunft. GA 193, Dornach 2007 (English edition: *Problems of Society*, Rudolf Steiner Press 2015); *Die Sendung Michaels. Die Offenbarung der eigentlichen Geheimnisse des Menschenwesens.* GA 194 (English edition: *Michael's Mission*, SteinerBooks 2015); and Thomas Meyer (editor): *Rudolf Steiner. Die Vorträge über Ahrimans Inkarnation im Westen aus dem Jahre 1919* ('Rudolf Steiner—lectures in the year 1919 on Ahriman's incarnation in the west'). Basel 2016.

12   See Rudolf Steiner: *Soziales Verständnis aus geisteswissenschatlicher Erkenntnis. Die geistigen Hintergründe der sozialen Frage, Volume III.* GA 191. Dornach 1989, page 198. (English edition: *Understanding Society Through Spiritual-Scientific Knowledge*, op. cit.)

13   Rudolf Steiner: *Der innere Aspekt des sozialen Rätsels. Luziferische Vergangenheit und ahrimanische Zukunft.* GA 193. Dornach 2007, page 186. (English edition: *Problems of Society*, op. cit.)

14   Ibid. page 185.

15   Ibid.

16   Ibid. page 164.

17   Ibid. page 194.

18   Rudolf Steiner: *Weltsilvester und Neujahrsgedanken.* GA 195, page 54. (English edition: *Cosmic New Year*, op. cit.)

19   Rudolf Steiner: *Der innere Aspekt des sozialen Rätsels. Luziferische Vergangenheit und ahrimanische Zukunft.* GA 193, page 54. (English edition: *Problems of Society*, op. cit.)

20   See Rudolf Steiner: *Soziales Verständnis aus geisteswissenschaftlicher Erkenntnis. Die geistigen Hintergründe der sozialen Frage, Volume III.* GA 191, page 199. (English edition: *Understanding Society Through Spiritual-Scientific Knowledge*, op. cit.).

21   Rudolf Steiner: *Der innere Aspekt des sozialen Rätsels. Luziferische Vergangenheit und ahrimanische Zukunft.* GA 193, page 170. (English edition: *Problems of Society*, op. cit.)

22   Ibid. page 167.

23   Ibid. page 174.

24   See Rudolf Steiner: *Soziales Verständnis aus geisteswissenschaftlicher Erkenntnis. Die geistigen Hintergründe der sozialen Frage, Volume III.* GA 191, page 208. (English edition: *Understanding Society Through Spiritual-Scientific Knowledge*, op. cit.)

25　Rudolf Steiner: *Der innere Aspekt des sozialen Rätsels. Luziferische Vergangenheit und ahrimanische Zukunft.* GA 193, page 194. (English edition: *Problems of Society*, op. cit.)

26　Ibid. page 177.

27　Ibid. page 172.

28　See Rudolf Steiner: *Soziales Verständnis aus geisteswissenschaftlicher Erkenntnis. Die geistigen Hintergründe der sozialen Frage, Volume III.* GA 191, page 203. (English edition: *Understanding Society Through Spiritual-Scientific Knowledge*, op. cit.)

29　Ibid. page 210.

30　Rudolf Steiner: *Der innere Aspekt des sozialen Rätsels. Luziferische Vergangenheit und ahrimanische Zukunft.* GA 193, page 191. (English edition: *Problems of Society*, op. cit.)

31　Ibid. page 192.

32　Rudolf Steiner: *Weltsilvester und Neujahrsgedanken.* GA 195, page 57. (English edition: *Cosmic New Year*, op. cit.)

33　See Rudolf Steiner: *Soziales Verständnis aus geisteswissenschaftlicher Erkenntnis. Die geistigen Hintergründe der sozialen Frage, Volume III.* GA 191, page 213. (English edition: *Understanding Society Through Spiritual-Scientific Knowledge*, op. cit.)

34　Ibid. page 202.

35　Rudolf Steiner: *Der innere Aspekt des sozialen Rätsels. Luziferische Vergangenheit und ahrimanische Zukunft.* GA 193, page 177. (English edition: *Problems of Society*, op. cit.)

36　Ibid. page 166.

37　Ibid. page 187.

38　Ibid. page 196.

39　Rudolf Steiner: *Weltsilvester und Neujahrsgedanken.* GA 195, page 39. (English edition: *Cosmic New Year*, op. cit.)

40　Ibid. page 53.

41　Ibid. page 54.

42　Rudolf Steiner: *Der innere Aspekt des sozialen Rätsels. Luziferische Vergangenheit und ahrimanische Zukunft.* GA 193, page 167. (English edition: *Problems of Society*, op. cit.)

43　See Rudolf Steiner: *Soziales Verständnis aus geisteswissenschaftlicher Erkenntnis. Die geistigen Hintergründe der sozialen Frage, Volume III.* GA 191, page 219. (English edition: *Understanding Society Through Spiritual-Scientific Knowledge*, op. cit.)

44   Ibid. page 220.
45   Rudolf Steiner: *Der innere Aspekt des sozialen Rätsels. Luziferische Vergangenheit und ahrimanische Zukunft.* GA 193, page 178. (English edition: *Problems of Society*, op. cit.)
46   See Peter Selg: *Elisabeth Vreede, Adversity, Resilience and Spiritual Science*, SteinerBooks 2017.
47   See Rudolf Steiner: *Soziales Verständnis aus geisteswissenschaftlicher Erkenntnis. Die geistigen Hintergründe der sozialen Frage, Volume III.* GA 191, page 200. (English edition: *Understanding Society Through Spiritual-Scientific Knowledge*, op. cit.)
48   Ibid. page 220.
49   Ibid. page 275.
50   Rudolf Steiner: *Der innere Aspekt des sozialen Rätsels. Luziferische Vergangenheit und ahrimanische Zukunft.* GA 193, page 188. (English edition: *Problems of Society*, op. cit.)
51   Ibid. page 187.
52   Ibid. page 195.
53   Rudolf Steiner: *Vier Mysteriendramen (Four Mystery Dramas).* GA 14, page 257.
54   See, among other: Gundhild Kacer-Bock: *Die Mysteriendramen im Lebensgang Rudolf Steiners* ('The mystery dramas in the course of Rudolf Steiner's life'), Stuggtart 2008; Manfred Krüger: *Mysteriendramatik im Seelenraum* ('The drama of mysteries in the soul'), Dornach 2008; Wilfried Hammacher: *Die Uraufführung der Mysteriendramen von und durch Rudolf Steiner—München 1910-1913* ('The première performance of the Mystery Dramas by Rudolf Steiner—Munich 1910-1913'), Dornach 2010; Peter Selg: *Esoterische Gemeinschaften in Rudolf Steiners Mysteriendramen* ('Esoteric communities in Rudolf Steiner's Mystery Dramas'), Arlesheim 2010.
55   Rudofl Steiner: *Vier Mysteriendramen (Four Mystery Dramas)*, GA 14, page 534.
56   Ibid. page 302.
57   Ibid. page 70.
58   Ibid. page 305.
59   Ibid. page 255.
60   Ibid. page 257.
61   Ibid. page 258.
62   Ibid. page 375.

63   Ibid.
64   Ibid. page 263.
65   Ibid. page 365.
66   Ibid. page 363.
67   Ibid. page 517.
68   Ibid. page 391.
69   Ibid. page 371.
70   Ibid. page 514.
71   Ibid. page 516.
72   Ibid. page 445.
73   Ibid. page 531.
74   Ibid. page 533.
75   Ibid. page 534.
76   Rudolf Steiner: *Unsere Toten. Ansprachen, Gedenkworte und Medita-tionssprüche 1905-1924*. GA 261, Dornach 1984, page 40. (English edition: *Our Dead—Memorial, Funeral, and Cremation Addresses*, SteinerBooks 2011.)
77   Rudolf Steiner: *Wege un Ziele des geistigen Menschen*, GA 125, Dornach 1984, page 40. (English edition: *Paths and Goals of the Spiritual Human Being*, Rudolf Steiner Press 2015.)
78   Karl Jaspers: *Der philosophische Glaube* ('Philosophical belief'). Zurich 1948, p 55. Quoted by Thomas Fuchs in *Verteidigung des Menschen. Grundfragen einer verkörperten Anthropologie* ('The defence of humanity. Basic questions of an epitomized anthropology') Berlin 2020, page 7.
79   Rudolf Steiner: *Bilder okkulter Siegel und Säulen. Der Münchner Kongress Pfingsten 1907 und seine Auswirkungen*. GA 284. Dornach 1993, p. 168. (English edition: *Rosicrucianism Renewed*, SteinerBooks 2007.)
80   Rudolf Steiner: *Anthroposophische Leitsätze. Der Erkenntnisweg der Anthroposophie—Das Michael-Mysterium*. GA 26. Dornach 10 1998, p. 84. (English edition: *Anthroposophical Leading Thoughts*, Rudolf Steiner Press 1998.)
81   Ibid. page 91.
82   Ibid. page 97.
83   Ibid. page 86.
84   Ibid. page 91.
85   Sergei O. Prokofieff: *Anthroposophy and 'The Philosophy of Freedom'*, Temple Lodge Publishing 2009.

86   Rudolf Steiner: *Anthroposophische Leitsätze. Der Erkenntnisweg der Anthroposophie—Das Michael-Mysterium.* GA 26, p. 93. (English edition: *Anthroposophical Leading Thoughts*, op. cit.)

87   Ibid. page 97.

88   Ibid. page 101.

89   Ibid. page 97ff.

90   Ibid. page 110.

91   Ibid. page 112.

92   Ibid. page 104ff.

93   Ibid. page 114ff.

94   Ibid. page 256.

95   Rudolf Steiner: *Menschenschicksale und Völkerschicksale.* GA 157. Dornach 1981, p. 106. (English edition: *Destinies of Individuals and Nations*, Rudolf Steiner Press 1986.)

96   Ibid. page 110.

97   Rudolf Steiner: *Anthroposophische Leitsätze. Der Erkenntnisweg der Anthroposophie – Das Michael-Mysterium.* GA 26, p. 257. (English edition: *Anthroposophical Leading Thoughts*, op. cit.)

98   See particularly Clemens G. Arvay: *Wir können es besser. Wie Umweltzerstörung die Corona-Pandemie auslöste und warum ökologische Medizin unsere Rettung ist.* ('We can do better. How destruction of the environment caused the corona pandemic and why ecological medicine is our slavation.')

99   Klaus Schwab and Thierry Malleret: *Covid-19: Der große Umbruch.* Cologny/Genf. 2020, p. 97. (All quotations in this book are taken from the original English edition: *Covid-19, The Great Reset*, Agentur Schweiz 2020.)

100 Ibid. page 102ff.

101 Ibid. page 148.

102 Ibid. page 154.

103 Ibid. page 12.

104 Ibid. page 22.

105 see also Hannes Hofbauer/Sefan Kraft (ed.): *Lockdown 2020. Wie ein Virus dazu benutzt wird, die Gesellschaft zu verändern.* ('Lockdown 2020 : how a virus is being used to change society').

106 Klaus Schwab and Thierry Malleret: *Covid-19: Der große Umbruch.* Cologny/Genf. 2020, p. 16 and 296. (English edition: *Covid-19, The Great Reset*, op. cit.)

107   Ibid. page 204.

108   Ibid. page 298.

109   Ibid. page 20.

110   Ibid. page 147ff.

111   Ibid. page 259. It is interesting to follow closely how the developments Schwab and Malleret describe in their book, and strongly support, are constantly interspersed with warnings about, among other things, surveillance and manipulation and the loss of individual freedoms; also to follow paragraph after paragraph of their criticism of the management of the Coronavirus (not only in their relativizing of the 'killier virus' mystique but also their questioning of media obsession, its problematizing of the psychological damage and the evocation of fear etc.); and how much weight they give to the ecological aspects of the crisis in order later on to bring these problems into their technological solution strategies (see note 129).

112   Ibid. page 253.

113   Ibid. page 251ff.

114   https://www.facebook.com/worldeconomic-forum/videos/189569908956561.

115   Klaus Schwab and Thierry Malleret: *Covid-19: Der große Umbruch*. Cologny/Genf. 2020, page 244. (English edition: *Covid-19, The Great Reset*, op. cit.)

116   Paul Schreyer: *Chronik einer angekündigten Krise. Wie ein Virus die Welt verändern konnte* ('Account of a forecast crisis—how a virus was able to change the world'). Berlin 2020, page 51.

117   Ibid. page 40.

118   Ibid. page 56.

119   Ibid. page 46.

120   Ibid. page 58.

121   Ibid. page 58f.

122   Ibid. page 160.

123   Ibid. page 160.

124   Klaus Schwab and Thierry Malleret: *Covid-19: Der große Umbruch*, page 179.

125   Ibid. page 153.

126   Paul Schreyer: *Chronik einer angekündigten Krise. Wie ein Virus die Welt verändern konnte* ('Account of a forecast crisis—how a virus was able to change the world'), page 51.

127 Sascha Lobo: *Realitätsschock. Zehn Lehren aus der Gegenwart* ('The shock of reality: ten lessons from the present') Cologne 2019, page 197.
128 Klaus Schwab and Thierry Malleret: *Covid-19: Der große Umbruch,* page 192.
129 Ibid. page 194.
130 Ibid. page 198f.
131 Page 210.
132 Ibid. page 241.
133 Ibid. page 243. Schwab and Malleret then continue their technological vision of the future with regards to the collection of personal data—'in combination with AI, the Internet of Things, monitors and wearable technology'—with an apparent 'ecological' slant, with these words: 'In the post-COVID-19 world, precise information on our carbon footprints, our impact on biodiversity, on the toxicity of all the ingredients we consume and the environments or spatial contexts in which we evolve will generate significant progress in terms of our awareness of collective and individual well-being.' (Ibid. page 244.)
134 Ibid. page 195.
135 Sascha Lobo: *Realitätsschock. Zehn Lehren aus der Gegenwart* ('The shock of reality: ten lessons from the present') Cologne 2019, page 201.
136 Ibid. page 203.
137 Ibid. page 208.
138 Ibid. page 209.
139 Ibid. page 211.
140 See Klaus Schwab and Thierry Malleret: *Covid-19: Der große Umbruch),* page 198ff.
141 Ibid.
142 Thomas Fuchs in *Verteidigung des Menschen. Grundfragen einer verkörperten Anthropologie.* ('The defence of humanity. Basic questions of an epitomized anthropology') Berlin 2020, page 9. For Fuchs' discussion regarding Harari in his book *Homo Deus,* see ibid. page 9ff.
143 Ibid. page 31.
144 Ibid. page 10.

145 Rudolf Steiner: *Der innere Aspekt des sozialen Rätsels. Luziferische Vergangenheit und ahrimanische Zukunft.* GA 193, page 174. (English edition: *Problems of Society,* op. cit.)

146 Thomas Fuchs in *Verteidigung des Menschen. Grundfragen einer verkörperten Anthropologie.* ('The defence of humanity. Basic questions of an epitomized anthropology') page 84.

147 Ibid. page 17.

148 Rudolf Steiner: *Gegensätze in der Menschheitsentwicklung. West und Ost—Materialismus und Mystik—Wissen und Glauben.* GA 197. Dornach 1996, page 164. (English edition: *Polarities in the Evolution of Mankind. West and East, Materialism and Mysticism, Knowledge and Belief,* Rudolf Steiner Press 1987.)

149 Rudolf Steiner: *Vier Mysteriendramen (Four Mystery Dramas).* GA 14, page 73.

150 Thomas Fuchs in *Verteidigung des Menschen. Grundfragen einer verkörperten Anthropologie.* ('The defence of humanity. Basic questions of an epitomized anthropology') page 17.

151 Ibid. page 34.

152 Ibid. page 64.

153 Klaus Schwab and Thierry Malleret: *Covid-19: Der große Umbruch,* page 62.

154 Ibid. page 210.

155 Klaus Schwab and Thierry Malleret: *Covid-19: Der große Umbruch,* page 179.

156 Rudolf Steiner: *Vier Mysteriendramen (Four Mystery Dramas).* GA 14, page 284.

157 See Peter Selg: *The Mystery of the Earth, Essays in the Time of Coronavirus,* SteinerBooks 2021.

158 Notebook no. 41, Rudolf Steiner Archiv, Dornach.

159 Rudolf Steiner: *Vier Mysteriendramen (Four Mystery Dramas).* GA 14, page 521.

160 Rudolf Steiner: *Gegenwärtiges und Vergangenes im Menschengeiste.* GA 167. Dornach 2 1962, page 100. (English edition: *The Human Spirit,* Rudolf Steiner Press 2015.)

161 Rudolf Steiner: *Der innere Aspekt des sozialen Rätsels. Luziferische Vergangenheit und ahrimanische Zukunft.* GA 193, page 66. (English edition: *Problems of Society,* op. cit.)

162 Rudolf Steiner: *Soziales Verständnis aus geisteswissen-schaftlicher Erkenntnis. Die geistigen Hintergründe der sozialen Frage*, Volume III. GA 191, page 212. (English edition: *Understanding Society Through Spiritual-Scientific Knowledge*, op. cit.)

163 Rudolf Steiner: *Vier Mysteriendramen (Four Mystery Dramas)*. GA 14, page 370.

164 Rudolf Steiner: *Soziales Verständnis aus geisteswissen-schaftlicher Erkenntnis. Die geistigen Hintergründe der sozialen Frage*, Volume III. GA 191, page 274. (English edition: *Understanding Society Through Spiritual-Scientific Knowledge*, op. cit.)

165 Rudolf Steiner: *Vier Mysteriendramen (Four Mystery Dramas)*. GA 14, page 535.

166 See Peter Selg: *Die Zukunft der Erde. Franz von Assisi, die Rosenkreuzer und die Anthroposophie* ('The Future of the Earth. Francis of Assisi, the Rosicrucians and Anthroposophy'). Arlesheim 2021.

167 Rudolf Steiner: *Vier Mysteriendramen (Four Mystery Dramas)*. GA 14, page 409.

168 Rudolf Steiner: *Soziales Verständnis aus geisteswissen-schaftlicher Erkenntnis. Die geistigen Hintergründe der sozialen Frage*, Volume III. GA 191, page 275. (English edition: *Understanding Society Through Spiritual-Scientific Knowledge*, op. cit.)

169 See Peter Selg: *Der Untergang des Abendlands? Rudolf Steiners Auseinandersetzung mit Oswald Spengler* ('The demise of the Occident? Rudolf Steiner's dispute with Oswald Spengler'). Arlesheim and Dornach 2020.

170 Rudolf Steiner: *Geisteswissenschaft als Erkenntnis der Grundimpulse sozialer Gestaltung*. GA 199. Dornach 1985, page 223. (English edition: *Spiritual Science as a Foundation for Social Forms*, Rudolf Steiner Press 1986.)

171 Rudolf Steiner: *Menschenwerden, Weltenseele und Weltengeist— Zweiter Teil: Der Mensch als geistiges Wesen im historischen Werdegang*. GA 206. Dornach 1991, page 92. (English edition: *Cosmosophy*, Vol. 1, Anthroposophic Press 1985.)

172 Rudolf Steiner: *Vier Mysteriendramen (Four Mystery Dramas)*. GA 14, page 438.

173 Rudolf Steiner: *Die Sendung Michaels. Die Offenbarung der eigentlichen Geheimnisse des Menschenwesens*. GA 194, page 26. (English edition: *Michael's Mission*, op. cit.)

174   Rudolf Steiner: *Vorträge und Kurse über christlich-religiöses Wirken, IV. Vom Wesen des wirkenden Wortes* ('Lectures and courses on Christian religion, IV. On the nature of the working of the Word'). GA 345. Dornach 1994, page 78.

175   Rudolf Steiner: *Der Tod als Lebenswandlung*. GA 182. Dornach 1996, page 183. (English edition: *Death as a Metamorphosis of Life*, Steiner-Books 2008.)

176   Friedrich Doldinger: *Die Ewige Stadt* ('The eternal city'). Freiburg 1946, page 111. In this connection see also the new edition of Thomas Kivelitz (Stuttgart 1997) and Peter Selg: *Apokalypse. Vom Weg zur Ewigen Stadt* ('Apocalypse. The path to the Eternal City'). Arlesheim 2020.

Wende-Zeit ist gekommen!
Es beben alle bergenden Hütten und Hüllen.
Und wer nicht wachsen will,
den zerschmettert der Schicksale Last.
Zu entschreiten dem Schrecknis,
nur dem Wachenden gelingt es,
der das Kommende
mit ganzer Kraft und Demut
innig empfängt.

A note from the publisher

For more than a quarter of a century, **Temple Lodge Publishing** has made available new thought, ideas and research in the field of spiritual science.

Anthroposophy, as founded by Rudolf Steiner (1861-1925), is commonly known today through its practical applications, principally in education (Steiner-Waldorf schools) and agriculture (biodynamic food and wine). But behind this outer activity stands the core discipline of spiritual science, which continues to be developed and updated. True science can never be static and anthroposophy is living knowledge.

Our list features some of the best contemporary spiritual-scientific work available today, as well as introductory titles. So, visit us online at **www.templelodge.com** and join our emailing list for news on new titles.

If you feel like supporting our work, you can do so by buying our books or making a direct donation (we are a non-profit/charitable organisation).

office@templelodge.com

TEMPLE LODGE

For the finest books of Science and Spirit